Bet
on
YOU

Bet
on
YOU

How to
WIN
with Risk

Angie Morgan
and Courtney Lynch

HarperCollins
LEADERSHIP

An Imprint of HarperCollins

Published by Harper Horizon, an imprint of
HarperCollins Focus LLC.

Any internet addresses, phone numbers, or company or
product information printed in this book are offered as a
resource and are not intended in any way to be or to imply
an endorsement by Harper Horizon, nor does
Harper Horizon vouch for the existence, content, or services
of these sites, phone numbers, companies, or products
beyond the life of this book.

ISBN 978-1-4002-2980-2 (eBook)

ISBN 978-1-4002-2979-6 (HC)

Library of Congress Control Number: 2021951250

Printed in the United States of America

22 23 24 25 26 LSC 10 9 8 7 6 5 4 3 2 1

To Ed, Judge, and Gardner.
May the risks we take together
continue to feel like amazing adventures.
—Angie

To Jamie and Tracie.
You have everything it takes to bet on you.
—Courtney

Contents

Section Three:
STAYING SAFE AND RECOGNIZING WINS

THE PLAY-IT-SAFE PARADOX

We're taught from a very young age to stay on the safe path. From the earliest moments in our lives, we've calibrated our behaviors with "no," "don't," and "stay away from..."— messages designed to keep us secure.

Then, through our preschool years and beyond, we heard fairy tales and nursery rhymes reinforcing these points.

Remember the tale of "Little Red Riding Hood"? The story about a girl who strayed off the path and talked to a stranger, which resulted in her near-death experience and the murder of her grandmother? Yeah, the moral of that story isn't subtle at all.

Once we graduated from story hour, we heard adages advocating security, "better safe than sorry," and idioms meant to keep us out of trouble, "curiosity *killed* the cat." We also listened to well-intentioned people tell us how to live cautiously, like when our parents pointed out which of our friends were bad seeds, and guidance counselors who encouraged us to apply to "safety schools" in the likely event that our post–high school dreams didn't come true.

All these lessons, at the time, were pretty valuable to us. If you've never touched a hot burner, taken candy from a stranger, or, on a more positive note, if you've ever lived out a pretty exciting Plan B experience, then you've been the fortunate recipient of some great life lessons.

There comes a time, though, when these messages stop helping. When we've developed the judgment to keep ourselves free from harm, and enacted agency and moved to the driver's seat of our own life, the lingering effect of consistent play-it-safe directions can block us from pursuing experiences that lead us toward the good life we envision for ourselves.

It's paradoxical, isn't it? The exact guidance that helped raise us to become successful adults is the exact guidance that could be holding us back from fulfilling our dreams.

We see the lasting effects of the play-it-safe mindset in nearly every adult leader we coach. As the founders of Lead Star, a successful leadership development consulting firm, we've spent nearly two decades supporting professionals by helping them develop their vision and leadership skills to increase their results. Our life's work is to help others succeed, and we've been fortunate to partner with great businesses like Google, Facebook, Walmart, and FedEx.

Like NFL quarterbacks who've watched thousands of hours of video to perfect their game-time, decision-making process, we've witnessed thousands of leaders make many choices. We've also had the opportunity to coach them through challenges, failures, setbacks, and missteps to help redirect them toward the greater successes they set out to achieve. Through the many leadership development journeys we've been privileged to guide, we've realized even the best leaders often lack the one critical skill set that *always* leads to breakthroughs:

The consistent ability to bet on themselves.

In *Bet on You*, we're going to help you understand the most common missing ingredient to a life well lived, one where you experience less stress, more success, and more joy. We've watched too many leaders struggle with unnecessary drama, angst, frustration, and lost happiness by not recognizing their true talents and, instead, defaulting to the play-it-safe mode they were raised to embrace.

The good news is that there's a way to counter our safety bias and build the bridge between where you are and where you want to be. It's through developing and embracing a skill set that you've probably paid little attention to before but is critical now, because it'll help you transform uncertainty into opportunity in every aspect of your life.

That skill set is knowing how to take risks.

RISK: THE MISSING INGREDIENT IN YOUR SUCCESS FORMULA

Risk is the missing ingredient in your formula for success, however you choose to define success:

- Investing in your continuing education
- Launching that side-hustle business that's been on your mind
- Moving from the city to the suburbs for a more balanced life
- Earning that promotion that seems out of reach
- Taking a career hiatus so you can live overseas
- Engaging more in making a difference in your community
- Starting a family during the peak season of your career

We understand it's likely that no one has ever told you risk-taking would be so critical on your life's journey. Believe us, no one ever told us either.

We were raised like you. We were taught how to play the security game and later were told that a good education, a network of friends, and landing a "good" job were all we needed to get ahead in life. No one ever sat us down and pushed this "risk-taking" message.

We stumbled upon it on our own volition when we both joined the Marine Corps, which is where our friendship was formed. Surprisingly, it wasn't the risky nature of military service that drew us in. It was something else—the call to be something more, to serve our country, to transform into better versions of ourselves (and a little money for school to boot). Little did we know when we signed up that we were about to get the master class "How to Take Risks."

After we left the Marines, we decided to join forces and take many more risks together. We started our business, Lead Star, in 2004 when we were both in our twenties and realized that the leadership lessons we learned in the Corps had so much value to every area of our lives. We also knew that most people have never really learned how to lead in such a practical way as we had, which is often the missing link that connects their talents, education, and desire to advance in their careers. We wanted to do something about this. So, we scraped together some of our savings, pulled out our credit cards to cover where our cash fell short, and started on our journey to build our firm and support professionals as they grew their leadership abilities.

We saw our business as an opportunity to share Marine Corps–inspired leadership lessons with as many people as possible to help them understand that leadership isn't a place on an organization chart; it's a behavior. It's the ability to influence outcomes and inspire others. Anyone at any level in a business can lead. When they do, good things happen to them—they build trust, they earn respect, and they're capable of transforming a group of individuals into a team.

We've also written two books on leadership, *Leading from the Front* and *SPARK*. Believe us—if there's a channel we can use to evangelize our message, we'll use it. Our passion has always been about helping people advance in ways they may never have considered before.

Bet on You is written in the same spirit. Our motivation is to help you be successful, and not just by improving your leadership skills. It's through developing a risk-taking mindset and the commensurate risk-taking skills to help you develop the courage to step toward whatever it is you've been wanting to do for a while but have hesitated to do.

RISK-TAKING ISN'T JUST FOR EPIC MOMENTS

Now, when we talk about risk, we're not talking big, scary, epic risks often associated with Marine Corps commercials—ones where you run toward the sound of chaos in full battle gear ready to engage in a gunfight and put yourself in physical danger. Rather, we learned about small, consistent risk-taking that helped us understand how to push ourselves out of our comfort zone a little more each day, how the impossible is probable with the right focus and daily commitment, and how to leverage the awesome and overwhelming power of teamwork to achieve whatever is on your heart and mind. (We can't underscore this enough—to do great things, you need a great support network!)

This is part of the risk-taking formula we're writing about in *Bet on You*—the same formula we've applied to every endeavor in our life that has led us to some pretty profound successes, like building a multimillion-dollar consulting firm, advising leaders at the world's best businesses, and, more important, designing our work life to support our whole lives. We take great pride in sharing that our career responsibilities have never pinned us down. Our business has always been geographically agnostic, allowing our families the good fortune of living in many fantastic places. We're so excited to share with you, too, how risk-taking will help you discover the joy, rewarding challenge, and adventure commensurate with living a life fully.

And we know we can't talk about risk by only focusing on the upside.

While you'll undoubtedly hear us express passionately the value risk-taking can bring to your life, we recognize that not every choice you make works out like you planned. (Let's be real—very few of them do.) There are times when taking a risk will lead you astray, and then there are others when taking risks can lead you to some glorious fails. In *Bet on You,* we're going to share with you many of our missteps and mistakes, which we're not afraid to expose. We share them candidly so you can get the benefit of our experience and, we hope, feel more comfortable about embracing your own. We know failure is never final, and past poor decisions shouldn't make you shrink when you contemplate future actions. Setbacks present powerful learning lessons that help you acquire wisdom and experience, qualities you can use to fast-track yourself forward.

We also know that, despite your best efforts and intentions, failure is nearly impossible to avoid. It's just one of those things in life that happens, whether you like it or not. We're here to advocate that it's better to fail when attempting something important that will allow you to grow than fail when you're not stretching at all. In other words, if you're going to fail—and you will—we want you to make it count and have a strategy in place to pull yourself up again so that you're stronger and more resilient because of the experience.

BET ON YOU: THE LIFE AND BUSINESS IMPERATIVE

So, it could very well be that, right now, where you sit, you're not contemplating something huge for yourself and in your life.

And that's okay. Change for change's sake is pointless. If you're content, then, please—go with it. *Bet on You* is still relevant.

During the global pandemic, many of us realized that what we've long considered our safety nets—an employer, a government, a retirement account, or even a family member—can't keep us safe from every threat we face. The only real security you have in life is something you've been building your entire career—your talent, one of the most important elements of your safety net. We know something about you that we feel compelled to share. When you couple your talent with an ability to take risks, you'll be prepared to manage effectively any external disruption that comes your way.

And here's something else—building the risk muscle will allow you to be a much stronger contributor in your role at work. Risk is, after all, an extremely high-value, in-demand competency that businesses are dying to develop among their employees. The World Economic Forum routinely surveys business leaders to ask what skills are required for the future of work. Increasingly, these leaders cite creativity, innovation, and complex problem-solving in our global workforce both now and in the future—skills that require the ability to take and manage risks. So, if you're ever sitting in a meeting with a great idea that you're hesitant to share, we want you to have the courage to share it, the confidence to believe that you can lead the effort, and the additional discipline to take action.

OUR JOURNEY TOGETHER

Bet on You is divided into three parts that focus on practical guidance to help you lead your life toward success and satisfaction:

Section One: Rethinking Risk

We'll demystify risk-taking so you can evolve your understanding of this concept and its nature. Risk is often mistakenly pitted against reward, as if there are only two options when you decide to take a chance on yourself. This type of binary, win–lose setup really narrows our view on what is true risk-taking. And, it can often prevent you from seeing how you have the ability to meet a challenge head on and lead through it well.

Section Two: Defining Success and Doing the Work

Here we'll provide you with step-by-step guidance on how to enact change, through risk-taking, in very thoughtful, incremental ways. Doing this certainly requires you to dream big, yet we'll help you level up the quality of your dreams since we know frivolous dreams contain little guidance for action.

Keep in mind, too, that we don't advocate for taking careless risks; we want you to move forward in your life in ways that honor your goals and aspirations. We also want you to do so in a measured way. Lasting, sustainable change takes time and discipline. It should be accompanied by joy and satisfaction. You're more likely to realize your dreams when you're having a good time along the way. We'll help you unpack what you want out of life in multidimensional ways so that your hard work adds up to something significant. We'll also help you identify from whom you'll need support. The right guide, at the right time, can accelerate your success.

Section Three: Staying Safe and Recognizing Wins

Weaving a strong safety net is a key factor in building the confidence to leverage risk consistently. We'll show you how to do this. And, we'll also help you recognize your wins. We've seen far too many professionals jump on an achievement treadmill, seeking success after success to their own detriment. We ourselves have fallen into this achievement trap. While it might seem counterintuitive, we have to learn to recognize when we're achieving progress so that we can both savor the sweetness of victory and use that experience to realize our growth and expanding capabilities. If we don't see our talents for what they are, we'll believe we don't have what it takes to follow through on our intentions for our lives.

YOUR PERSONAL RISK MANIFESTO

Most professionals recognize that achieving their dreams takes hard work and dedication. We agree. What it doesn't require is years of delay before building up the courage to live a life that's meaningful and fulfilling to you. In *Bet on You,* we're going to focus on you and the urgency around why now is the time to step toward your vision. We'll help you rightsize risk by sharing that it's really just a decision that, when followed by action, gets you started down a path of growth and development.

We want you to succeed because we know you can. To do so, we're going to set you up with a step-by-step risk-taking plan. Throughout this book you'll find opportunities to complete brief, online exercises. We encourage you to do those as you experience each chapter. When you do, you'll finish this book with your personal Risk Manifesto, a detailed plan for winning with risk in your life. Reading is valuable, but reflection and action are far more important. We want you to use the online portal to ensure you're taking every advantage to leverage risk for success in your life.

THIS IS THE POINT

Many books tell great stories. Ours is different. Sure, we hope to tell great stories throughout *Bet on You*—not just ours, but of both famous and lesser-known leaders whose life examples can illuminate great lessons and serve as powerful testaments to the power of risk-taking.

Our book, though, is more like a mission.

We're zealous about the value of risk. We've experienced its value in so many ways. We weren't privileged kids who had inheritances that helped us advance in life. We're public school girls who had just enough moxie to think we could be Marines. From this transformative experience, we picked up a skill set that was the catalyst for every great thing that has happened in our lives. We don't want to keep what we know about risk a secret. We want you to know about it, to experience it, so you can get to that *better* in your life—a better career, a better balance between work and life, better relationships, and a better future. We know that *better* can be achieved if you do just one simple thing, time after time: *Bet on You.*

Section One

RETHINKING RISK

CHAPTER ONE

REIMAGINING RISK

"Everything is a risk. Not doing anything is a risk. It's up to you."

—NICOLA YOON[1]

QUICK LOOK

This chapter is about resetting your relationship with risk and understanding how you can use this winning quality to achieve success that matters to you.

THOUGHT STARTERS

Risk is the only path that leads to growth, opportunity, self-direction, transformation, and positive change.

Risk done right is a series of steps—one, followed by many more, that are measured, thoughtful, intentional, well-planned, and require incremental action, not sudden jumps.

Being open to a journey where uncertainty abounds can deliver far more wonderful and enriching experiences than you ever could imagine.

We define risk as taking action in the face of uncertainty. Since none of us can predict the future, that means risk and uncertainty are always fully present in our lives. You begin to grow comfortable with the concept of risk-taking when you acknowledge this truth. It will help you be more open to inviting risk into your life strategically, instead of working continuously to eliminate it.

Taking a risk is a conscious choice that allows you to move forward in life, versus being at the mercy of externalities. While it's a common notion to think of risk as the downside of a choice, the reality is that the outcomes of your risks can either be negative or positive, and not necessarily immediate. Choices you make today may lead to opportunities that won't surface until some point in the future. In fact, taking small risks today can be one of the greatest investments you make for your future.

And, unlike a gamble, where the odds favor the house, we believe that when you take risks, you influence your life so that the odds for success are far more in your favor. Additionally, any negative outcome often equates to an enriching experience that leads to learning and growth. Failure is only fatal when you stop growing; while it can be a setback, it can also be an experience that helps you acquire important lessons learned. After all, think about your life. What's been the better teacher: your failures, or your successes? Failures, right? We all know this intuitively, yet, for some reason, the logic isn't quite compelling enough to push us out of our failure-prevention mode.

Helping leaders reimagine risk is one of the most important things we do as coaches. We take the responsibility of helping others reframe their relationship seriously, because we've seen that the decision to not embrace daily risk-taking could actually be one of the greatest risks people take in their lives.

Warming up to risk can be difficult because the word *risk* is often used synonymously with danger, peril, liability, or threat. However, these words represent only one narrow side of the story. Another more essential, yet underrepresented, side of risk is that it's the only path that leads to growth, opportunity, self-direction, transformation, and positive change—all experiences that are possible and attainable by you.

Without comfort with risk, when uncertainty rears its ugly head, you could be making decisions out of desperate fear versus confident strength. It's like staying in a job you're unhappy with, then one day hearing the news that you're being let go. You could've made a thoughtful pivot into a better opportunity upon realizing the job wasn't for you, but instead you find yourself scrambling in response and running the chance of a lower salary and underemployment.

No one wants to be in that position, yet it's an unfortunate truth that many find themselves at a disadvantage due to their discomfort with both the concept of risk and the actual skills related to risk-taking. While it's clear we can't avoid taking risks, we can control the skill level we demonstrate in the face of it. By initiating risk-taking and inviting uncertainty into your life, you're in a better position to become more comfortable being uncomfortable, as well as influence your life's direction. One thoughtful risk will inevitably lead to another, and as you build your risk muscle, you'll be strengthening your risk capacity.

BALANCING RISK WITH
A KALEIDOSCOPE APPROACH

Can you remember marveling at a kaleidoscope when you were a kid? You'd hold up the lens, see brightly colored chips in a symmetrical pattern, and then with one twist of the scope you'd watch the chips tumble into a new, colorful, and balanced design.

What made the kaleidoscope mesmerizing was the right combination of chips in each equally sized chamber.

In the spirit of risk-taking, we'd like you to imagine each kaleidoscope chamber not only as elements of a well-lived life, but areas where you can direct your risk-taking to lead you toward the success you envision for yourself. Here are four common chambers that most men and women typically desire to enact risk in:

- **Risking in Life.** Some of the most important roles we fill—as partners, parents, and friends—allow us to grow our capacity for leveraging risk well.
- **Risking in Your Career.** Many of us spend more time on the job than in any other lane of our lives. Taking strategic risks at work builds skills and contributes to greater results.
- **Risking for Impact.** Serving others and our communities is one of the most important leadership roles we can have in our life.
- **Risking for Joy.** Finding fun, fulfillment, and satisfaction fuels our life journey. A life of little risk limits our opportunity for joy.

Throughout your *Bet on You* journey, you're going to read stories about risk-taking in each of these chambers to give you a stronger sense of areas in your life where you can exercise risk, too. As you reflect on these stories, you also might discover that you demonstrate risk with ease and comfort in one "chamber" but have a bit of a deficit in another chamber. We've seen this far too often:

- Our Marine colleagues who've taken extraordinary risks with their lives, but were extremely risk-averse when it came to investing in their education post-Corps.

- Friends who are outspoken in their community on issues they're passionate about but can't find the courage to negotiate a pay raise for themselves at work.
- Colleagues who'd take a promotion that compromises family time but won't change employers for a more flexible, family-friendly opportunity due to the disruption.

We'll show you that it's important to invite risk intentionally into your life when you can, because the experience you build by initiating risk-taking makes you even more ready for risk when it surprises you. This was the case with Courtney, when, early in her career, she attempted to channel the risk-taking mindset she applied in her career to her personal life.

RISKING IN LIFE: COURTNEY'S STORY

The Life-Enriching Element of Uncertainty

I'm a planner. I plan everything. So, when it came time to plan for a family, I have to admit I was pretty nervous about starting this journey. I knew my life was going to change dramatically, and I would cede some control to a marvelous, adorable little being. Yet, my husband Patrick and I knew we were ready to expand our family and invited the risk of welcoming a child into this world.

Lucky for us, it wasn't too long before I became pregnant.

Looking back, I don't remember much about the pregnancy before my first doctor visit. But I remember almost every detail about that first appointment.

Patrick and I drove to the doctor's office together, arriving early for my afternoon appointment. The waiting room was relatively empty. We left the magazines untouched as we waited for the nurse to call my name, chatting back and forth about our excitement. It wasn't a moment too soon when the door to the exam area opened and my name was called. We both followed the nurse back to an alcove where she took my vitals, weighed me in, and asked questions about my positive pregnancy test. Then, she led me to the sonogram room.

"Congratulations!" my doctor said as he shook Patrick's hand and gave me a hug. Then, he explained that the sonogram was a way of confirming the pregnancy and getting a more accurate estimate of the baby's due date. Soon the procedure was underway. After just a couple minutes, my doctor spoke up again, but it wasn't what I'd hoped to hear. He exclaimed, "Uh-oh!"

I panicked. *Uh-oh* wasn't what I was expecting. I knew that first pregnancies aren't always successful. And I was only about eight weeks along, which is a precarious time for any pregnancy. He must have seen the concerned look on my face, because he spoke again. "It's a good uh-oh, but I want to be absolutely sure before I say anything more. Just give me a couple minutes," he said as he continued to manipulate the dials on the ultrasound.

A good uh-oh? What could that be? I turned anxiously toward Patrick, who was standing by my side. I studied his navy blue shirt, a souvenir he'd picked up on one of our trips out West. It had images of Indian totem poles on it, each with a unique expression on its face. And just as Patrick and I made eye contact, both anxious for additional news, my doctor uttered a word that changed my perfectly planned efforts at starting a family completely. "Twins! You are having two babies, and they both look great! Strong heartbeats," he said as he raised the volume on the machine, allowing us to listen better. A life-changing moment for sure.

My parents and siblings, of course, got a huge kick out of this announcement when I shared the news. *The girl who plans for everything,* they shared, *couldn't possibly have planned for this.* And that's so true! I had no history of twins in my family. I later learned that I was having identical twins, which only happens in about one in 105 pregnancies. Modern medicine can't yet explain why identical twins happen. A perfectly healthy egg splits, and you end up with two babies instead of one. I've been told it's like winning the baby lottery. For me, however, as a first time, type A mother, it was pretty scary and intimidating.

Yet, many years later, I'm a proud, much more seasoned, twin mom. My daughters, Jessica and Kara, are still full of surprises. What surprised me, too, is how I've grown in my ability to love, parent, and support them. This totally unexpected twist in my parenting journey taught me so much about the joy of welcoming uncertainty into my life. It also highlighted the value of embracing risk consistently in thoughtful, well-balanced, and intentional ways. And, while you can only plan for so much, when you're risk ready what you don't plan for can present to you the most wonderful of experiences that enrich your life in ways you can't imagine.

THE THREE BIGGEST
MISCONCEPTIONS ABOUT RISK

We know that how we're talking about risk-taking isn't consistent with how it has likely been presented to you before picking up this book. To help you better understand the value of risk, we want to address the three biggest misconceptions about risk that are likely holding you back from embracing it well. We hope calling out these three commonly held beliefs will support you in reimagining risk as a powerful ingredient in your success formula.

Misconception 1: Risk Is the Opposite of Reward

Consider some of the best things that have happened to you in life. Perhaps they include some of these milestones: earning a degree, getting married, having children, earning a promotion, or winning a competition.

Now, think about this: None of these positive experiences would've happened if you didn't take a risk. In order to achieve any of these feats that you're proud of, you stepped into a world of tremendous uncertainty, one where the odds for success weren't guaranteed. Think for a second about going to college or getting married—the odds of success in either of these experiences are fifty-fifty. These odds aren't awesome, yet when people make decisions to move toward these pursuits, others are there to honor them with congratulatory gifts and send-off parties.

So, as you reflect on your life, it's clear you've definitely taken risks before. What's different, though, between risks of the past and risks you're hesitant to pursue right now? We'd argue that the ones you've already taken didn't feel like risks at the time because they were mainstream and popular—society-encouraged and mom-approved. Everyone else was doing it, so it felt safe.

The more experience we gain, the more unique our dreams and visions for our life become. We realize we have certain preferences and ideas we'd like to pursue. Those thoughts can include imagining different paths rather than some of the well-worn ones others have taken. Risks that appear unconventional or unlike more common milestones we seek to achieve can feel a little scarier, more dangerous. That's the Play-It-Safe Paradox happening in your life.

If we dare to imagine life a bit outside the acceptable norms of a "good future," our instincts can drive us to begin second-guessing ourselves or making a case why no action is for the best. Yet these authentic hopes for what we might do, become, or experience are likely very helpful indicators of where points of satisfaction, contribution, and fulfillment can be found. To build the steady courage needed to choose to step in directions that matter to you, you'll need to recalibrate your thinking about risk.

Rather than believe that risk is the opposite of reward, we want you to think of it as the path to reward. Now, it's not a smooth path, a clear path, or even a direct route. It's like the yellow brick road—a path that promises you adventure, the opportunity to meet some exciting companions, some obstacles that you'll have to overcome. In the end, you discover that you, like Dorothy, have, or can get, what you need to achieve what you want. You just have to believe that your talents, capabilities, and past risk-taking performance are great indicators of your future risk-taking success.

Once Angie's friend, Katy Bertodatto, realized she needed to bet on herself to experience the success she wanted in her life, she began following a path to reward that was filled with great challenge. Each challenge she overcame led to better and better results. Her journey shows us what is possible when we reimagine risk.

RISKING IN LIFE AND CAREER: KATY BERTODATTO

Risk-Taking, One Mile at a Time

When Katy finalized her divorce, she had twelve dollars in her bank account and two young sons to care for. She was waitressing at a bar at the time, which allowed her to make ends meet, but she knew it wasn't going to lead her and her boys to a life where they could do the simple things—take vacations, go out to eat, or even have a home of their own. She saw clearly that if she wanted to change her circumstances, she'd have to do something bold to level up. For her, that meant going back to college.

Taking on student debt was frightening for her because, if it didn't work out, she'd be worse off than when she started. Yet, she held the belief that she had to move forward—there was no going back. Finding the working, studying, and parenting groove was definitely difficult at first, but over time she earned an associate degree at her local community college.

Fueled by her accomplishment, she kept stepping forward, applying to four-year institutions throughout her state of Michigan. Much to her surprise, she was accepted at the one she coveted the most, the University of Michigan. What's more, when she received her acceptance letter, she also got notice that she had a full ride and housing benefits, for which she thanks her "low-income, single-mom status combined with my rock-solid high school and community college grade-point average."

Katy worked out a makeshift custody calendar with her ex-husband, and also attempted to arrange two households—one with her boys, and one in Ann Arbor, which was four hours away. For two years every Monday morning, Katy would wake up at 3:00 a.m. and head downstate so she could arrive early to her 8:30 class. She'd then stay at school until noon on Thursday, where she'd run from her class to her car so she could be back in Northern Michigan to pick up her boys after their school day.

Throughout this period, she encountered inevitable hiccups and barriers, some that felt insurmountable at times—a custody battle, housing disruptions, and self-doubt among them. Yet, Katy persevered. In all, she racked up more than thirty thousand miles on her car odometer in pursuit of her degree. When graduation day came, she was excited to accept her diploma in front of her children. Her classmates, inspired by her story, chose her to speak at the ceremony—an audience of more than ten thousand graduates and family members. She shared that not only would her education help her create a better life for her boys, she realized that without the lessons and experiences she acquired while exercising risk and the comfort she's developed with uncertainty, she wouldn't have made it as a nontraditional student.

Katy now owns a property management business, takes amazing vacations with her family, lives in a beautiful home in a resort community, and, ultimately, is in a far greater position to lead her life on her terms. She reminds herself frequently that if she could bet on herself with twelve dollars in the bank, then there was very little in life she couldn't overcome with focus, commitment, and the ability to leverage her risk-taking skills.

Misconception 2: Risk Is a Leap

Our society celebrates sudden, dramatic changes—*90 Day Fiancé,* anyone? You've also heard these chants and calls to action: Take the leap! Rip the Band-Aid off! Quit your job and change your life!

When it comes to taking a risk that is meaningful to you, don't follow any of this advice.

Risk done right is a series of steps—one, followed by many more—that are measured, thoughtful, intentional, well-planned, and require incremental action, not sudden jumps.

Bold, jarring, risk-taking moves often lead to less-than-best outcomes. We can see this sometimes in our impulsive choices, often driven by emotion void of logic. If you've ever bought a puppy on a whim or purchased exercise equipment that you saw late one night on an infomercial, then you know what we're talking about.

Creating intention means we've engaged our thought process, which helps us develop ideas for the type of change we want to see in our life. These thoughts become beliefs, which become behaviors. This formula lays the foundation for any lasting, sustainable change, which helps you achieve success while mitigating negative outcomes that could come your way.

We know of many self-led change initiatives that are flawed in design because they don't follow this formula. They start with behaviors, without giving the opportunity much thought. It's like starting a diet on a whim, but not choosing a program or method to follow. Or buying a camera because you want to study photography, and then realizing you just aren't willing to make the time to attend classes.

We often observe this trend, too, among our high-performing coaching clients who get contacted by headhunters. Our clients often aren't looking to change jobs, but they're intrigued to hear from someone—a stranger, nonetheless—that it's time for a change. These individuals get excited because it's something new, something different, and it's flattering for them to have their talents distinguished by an outside third party, so much so that they contemplate significant change—like moving their family cross-country or accepting a role that adds forty-five minutes one way to their commute—without thinking it through first.

Now, we'll be the first to say that headhunters fill a very important role. We know many great ones, as well as people who've used them to find incredible opportunities. Yet, our guidance to the men and women we coach is always the same: The best way to take a risk is, first, to decide that you want to make a change, and then use the resources available to you as you enact change methodically. Let the decision to change drive your next actions, rather than being pushed into change because an opportunity appears magically.

We learned a saying in the Marines that has been invaluable to us whenever we contemplate taking action toward something new: Slow is smooth, and smooth is fast. Whenever we start something that we've never done before, we need to approach it slowly, work out the kinks, and understand and appreciate what the opportunity requires from us. This knowledge allows us to pick up speed later, helping us reach our goal—in the end—more efficiently and with less headache.

So, when it comes to risk-taking, don't leap—step steadily and, before you know it, you'll be well on your way to the success you aspire to.

RISKING IN CAREER: REESE WITHERSPOON

If the Game's Not Working for You, Take a Risk to Change the Game

Reese Witherspoon is one of Hollywood's most beloved actresses. She consistently boasts one of the highest Q scores[2] based on her wide acclaim and likability. She started her film career at a very young age, sixteen, in the movie *Man on the Moon*. She then went on to star in many blockbuster successes, such as *Legally Blonde* and *Sweet Home Alabama*. At the age of twenty-nine, she earned an Oscar for her role as June Carter in the movie *Walk the Line*, a story about Johnny Cash's life. That's also when her career began to stall.

When she was thirty-six, *The New Yorker* added her to a list of what they considered has-been actors.[3] Reese was taken aback by what she believed was quite a premature death knell being sounded on her career. Yet it did serve as a wake-up call for her that she needed to be intentional about ushering in the next season of her career.

What's inspiring about what happened next was that, despite not getting interesting scripts or interesting roles, she decided to do something about it. Her proactive approach wasn't to double down on what anyone else would likely do in that situation—in other words, network more, accept an indie film at lesser pay so they could reintroduce themselves to the world, or be more demanding with their agent about getting better scripts. It was to reimagine the game she was playing.

Her husband, a talent agent at the time, observed that she loved to read and suggested that, rather than wait for the right parts to come to her, she should option the books she was reading, and develop the parts she wanted to perform. In other words, if the game's not working for you, change the game. She set to work diligently reviewing hundreds of titles for their possible production value. In 2016, her preparation and strategic career shift led her to create Hello Sunshine, her media company, which has since produced some pretty incredible hits (like the movie *Gone Girl* and the bingeworthy series *Big Little Lies*). Reese didn't stop there.

Hollywood is notorious for pay inequity among known and unknown actors, both men and women. Reese wanted to create a business focused on equity among those with whom she engaged, so, as she succeeded, others would, too. Unlike traditional Hollywood, which uses a standard, cutthroat, competitive model in all facets of business, Hello Sunshine promotes abundance and empowerment by being transparent about things like pay. The business also actively employs diversity on the set to ensure that a wide variety of talent is tapped.

Reese routinely extends her influence to relatively unknown authors, taking a chance on their work to help them break through to the mainstream. She also has book clubs available online to promote engagement and community.[4]

Reese Witherspoon is one person—one person whom some had called a has-been at thirty-six. In reality, she was just getting started. Reese epitomizes how to leverage risk to not only win for yourself, but help others win, too. She leveled up by betting on herself and taking a series of creative steps to design her life. It wasn't one leap that solidified her influence and leadership in Hollywood. Instead, she's made consistent, thoughtful choices that were right on time for her and the industry she works in.

Misconception 3: We Think We Can Avoid Taking Risks

Benjamin Franklin is famous for saying that the only certainties in life are death and taxes. This means that everything else in life is uncertain, and whenever there's uncertainty, there's risk.

For those who say they don't take risks, or state that they choose to avoid risks at all costs, we remind them that they may have a higher incidence of hidden risk in their lives without realizing it. For example:

- Coexisting in a toxic relationship (when the world is full of better, more inspiring people)
- Not scheduling an annual health checkup (when there's a family history of cancer or heart disease)
- Avoiding an uncomfortable conversation (while assuming that problems will just work themselves out)
- Having all their savings concentrated on their employer's stock purchase plan (and not diversifying their portfolio)
- Squandering their time on pursuits that don't connect to their values or priorities
- Missing out on the benefit of greater satisfaction and joy (by not following through on a goal that's meaningful to them)

We think we can avoid risk by building up our savings account, making smart employment moves, earning the "right" degree that connects directly to a job, or buying the safest car on the market, but the reality is that we can't hide from risk. The most we can do is mitigate it. The best we can do is embrace it.

RISK IS YOUR PATH TO GROWTH

Overriding your misconceptions about risk-taking allows you to enter a new era of growth and development for yourself.

Think of people you know who are taking risks and discovering new eras of success—your friend who opened a youth recreation league, your colleague who embraced the company's work-from-anywhere policy and now stays at Airbnbs in a different part of the country every quarter, or someone in your community who went into ministry to bring greater hope and inspiration into this world.

These examples reinforce, too, that when you're intentional about how you invite risk into your life, you improve your life and others notice and will inevitably be impacted. Whether you're aware of it or not, important people—like your children, your teammates, the team you lead, or the community in which you serve—are looking to you for guidance and inspiration. They take their cues from you. When you're invigorated, refreshed, and self-directed, they're moved and mirror what they see.

We've spent a lot of time in the past working directly with managers, helping them reengage their teams. These individuals come to us from a place of heartfelt sincerity and openness, seeking ways they can improve so they can get better and, in turn, help their teams get better. They not only want to step out onto a new path, but also want to use some tried, true, and tested actions that can help them get better efficiently. We're always honored to help. We warn them, though—it'll require them to do some things they've never done before, which is our not-so-secret code for taking risks.

What's always rewarding to see is how an ounce of risk sets into motion so much positive change, like with Craig.

RISKING IN CAREER: NEW WAYS OF WORKING DISCOVERED THROUGH RISK

Craig served as the dean at a small college. After attending one of our leadership development events, he decided to introduce leadership concepts to his fellow deans by inviting them to a monthly lunch-and-learn experience. The sessions had the simplest of designs—in advance of the meeting, he'd share a book excerpt or a TED talk or YouTube video on a leadership topic and ask everyone to engage in the content and bring ideas to discuss during the session. Then, when everyone was together, Craig facilitated a dialogue on the topic and ensured that everyone had a chance to share their thoughts and connect them to both their group and the work that they did.

Prior to these sessions, Craig shared that his colleagues often squabbled over resources, resisted collaboration on even simple ideas, and it felt like people were actively working against one another to build up their own department while breaking down others. He was amazed that, as he introduced these leadership concepts, like team trust, credibility, and accountability, both the conversation and cooperation among peers gradually shifted. The risk that he took—reimagining meetings and sharing new ideas—transformed his environment.

Your risks will transform yours, too, and will undoubtedly lead to your highest point of contribution, which we know is something we all strive to achieve.

Through our work at Lead Star, we've constantly reinforced the positive psychology message, a concept introduced by Dr. Abraham Maslow in his 1954 groundbreaking book, *Motivation and Personality*. Prior to his research, psychology centered on curing ailments, as well as negative aspects related to human shortcomings and illnesses. His work took a new twist and laid the foundation for some exciting research that helps us understand how we can all get better. By *better*, he means how we can all achieve a life worth living and self-actualize by realizing our talents and full potential.

We all can get better. By *better*, we don't mean that you need to get busier and do more. Sometimes, *better* is just reimagining where you are right now and how you can use every skill you have to take a new approach in life and embrace each day as a fresh opportunity to make your life work for you.

We know there's either a goal on your mind or a dream unpursued or even a move you've wanted to make for quite some time. What's been on your mind is far too important to be left to chance, and far too inspiring to delay another day. We believe you have everything you need to own this moment right now and to take the steps necessary to live your life the way you've envisioned it.

Sure, there will always be reasons why now isn't the right time or how next year could really be your year. But that style of thinking isn't going to help you lead your life and get to where you want to go. Quite the opposite. Thinking like that could steer you toward a future in which you look back at moments like these and say to yourself, "I wish I had . . .".

Study after study show that people who take risks are happier, more successful, and more fulfilled. We want this for you. We're excited about helping you understand how to embrace risk-taking to guide you toward your vision. As you grow more comfortable with inviting risk into your life, we want you to use it to make life work for you. And as you envision ways you can win with risk, we're 100 percent confident that the bets you make on yourself will pay off in ways you can't yet begin to imagine.

PUTTING IT INTO PRACTICE

- Start your personal Risk Manifesto at www.leadstar.us /bet-on-you. There you'll find brief, online exercises to support you in creating a detailed plan for winning with risk in your life.

- Reflect on your kaleidoscope and imagine ways you can create balance in your life through risk-taking.
- Seek to understand your misconceptions about risk and how they might be holding you back.
- Think about how you've been successful with risk in the past. Use these results to build confidence for new risks.
- Realize that the unique plans, visions, and goals you have for your life aren't wrong—they're important and need to be prioritized.
- Identify the hidden risks you're taking by not acting on your intentions.
- Imagine how your risk-taking can benefit others; use this as motivation as you continue your *Bet on You* journey.

CHAPTER TWO

IF NOT YOU, THEN WHO?

"The only person you are destined to become is the person you decide to be."

—JANET CHAMP AND CHARLOTTE MOORE,
1991 NIKE ADVERTISEMENT[1]

QUICK LOOK

This chapter helps you develop your perspective on yourself and your relationship with risk so you can move forward with a refreshed appreciation for your true capability.

THOUGHT STARTERS

To bet on you, you must know you and learn to trust yourself.

Risking is a learned behavior, meaning that you can redevelop a whole new relationship with it if you're not satisfied with the one you have.

Building confidence fuels your ability to take the risks that allow you to develop experiences that lead you toward the *better* you envision.

Quick Question: How old are you?

Whatever your answer to that question, that's the amount of time you've invested in getting to know yourself. No one should know you better than you.

And yet, in the same breath, we also have to ask: How well do you know you?

For the self-aware, they're real with themselves about who they are, and they accept the range of skills they've been blessed with. They know what they're really good at and, conversely, where they struggle. While they value external information about their talents and weaknesses, time only strengthens their ability to trust that they see themselves in a true light.

For those who've got some ground to cover on the self-awareness journey, that's the beauty of it all—it's a journey. This pursuit is worthwhile, rich, and never complete; all that's required is an open mind and curiosity around your strengths, gifts, areas that need to be developed, and opportunities to be explored.

While you build self-awareness, it's also important to consider what you're doing with the information that avails itself to you. Self-knowledge alone doesn't mean that you're headed on a course that's aligned to your interests, preferences, or values. We've met far too many great men and women who feel self-aware enough to know that they're either on the wrong course or living a life in pursuit of goals someone else established for them. Only risk-taking can help them—*and you*—course correct your future, ensuring that what matters to you most is expressed in your life fully, every day.

Self-awareness can be a very expansive topic, including subjects ranging from food preferences to how you handle confrontation. For the purpose of risk-taking, we want to home in on three critical areas that will support your risk-taking journey:

- Developing your self-reliance
- Understanding your risk disposition
- Actively building your confidence

YOU ARE YOUR OWN HERO

Are you familiar with the song "The Princess Who Saved Herself"? It's a catchy tune about a princess who decided not to wait for someone to rescue her. She took matters into her own hands by fending off a dragon and a witch, then later starting a band with them. The song was the brainchild of tech-guru-turned-musician Jonathan Coulton. While Coulton's genre was typically more rock and techno for adults, he took the opportunity to write a kids' song for a charity album to support youth in Haiti. He shared that his daughter was "obsessed with princesses, so I am forced to think and talk about them a lot. None of them really kick ass as much as I hope my daughter kicks ass when she's all grown up, so I made up one that does."[2]

Coulton's message is right on point for us all—prince, princesses, and commoners alike. No one is coming to save you. You've got everything inside of you to make things happen for you. Every time you "save" yourself, you get sharper, better, and stronger. In essence, you become more self-reliant.

Ralph Waldo Emerson, the early American writer and poet, introduced the concept of self-reliance to the general public in his 1841 essay titled, appropriately, "Self-Reliance," in which he shared that the best way to avoid conformity that's either self-imposed or society-imposed is by growing more aware of who you are and striving for your own goals, bravely.

We love that line—*striving for your own goals, bravely.* On your life's journey, undoubtedly people will have ideas and goals for you. While it can be helpful and useful to take input and recommendations from others, living an authentic life requires self-authorship of your own dreams and goals. That way, when you realize them, they'll feel right for you.

RISKING IN CAREER: DWAYNE JOHNSON

Even The Rock Has Doubts

Dwayne Johnson had to learn to trust himself early on in life as he faced challenges in navigating his career.[3] After failing to be drafted into the NFL post-college, and evaluating options like law school or joining the FBI, he decided to pursue a professional wrestling career like his father and grandfather.[4] Playing the character "Rocky Maivia," which was a combination of his father's and grandfather's ring names, Dwayne had one of the fastest rises as a rookie in the WWF (World Wrestling Federation, now known as the WWE [World Wrestling Entertainment]).

Billing him as the first third-generation wrestling sensation, WWF encouraged Dwayne to embrace a squeaky-clean, baby-faced image.[5] At first, fans loved him, and the WWF (which picked the winners of all wrestling matches ahead of time) chose him to win his first Survivor Series match. Then, just months later, it decided to award him the coveted Intercontinental Championship.[6]

During this period of Dwayne's early success, WWF's fan base was shifting. Clean-cut, good-guy characters were falling out of favor as the sport entered an "attitude era" when fans wanted tough outlaws to take the top prizes. Audiences began to turn against Rocky Maivia and his rapid rise, booing him at his post-championship appearances. The negativity got to Dwayne. Toward the end of the season, he was injured and returned home to rest and contemplate his future. Fearful that his wrestling career was ending as fast as his football career, he knew he needed to make some changes.

He met with WWF management, and they agreed to let him come back but told him they were placing him on the Nation of Domination—a team of rougher, tougher wrestlers. Dwayne realized this team was a better fit for who he really was. And, through playing the Rocky character, he knew fans just didn't buy him as the good guy. They, like him, wanted to cheer on a more authentic persona. Dwayne wanted to build a relationship with the audience not as a smiling good guy, but as who he really was, a tough competitor—positive on some days and ready to rumble on others.

The Rock was born soon after, and he went on to become one of the most successful wrestlers in the history of the industry. Through sheer self-reliance, and by stepping out of his father's and grandfather's identity, as well as shrugging off the character a company had created, Dwayne continued to build an exceptional career.

He once spoke of a personal low point he experienced in 2009, sharing that, "Professionally, I couldn't bet on myself. I wasn't used to that."[7] In response, he took a break. He realized that another reinvention was needed. Dwayne doubled down on who he was and painted a picture for his agents about the movie, fitness, and social media persona he wanted to become.

His agents didn't understand. He promptly changed management, deciding to bet on himself once again. Today, The Rock is an international sensation and recognized globally as a box office superstar. He personifies self-reliance and prides himself on always being the hardest working person in the room.

It's hard to believe that legends like The Rock experience the same type of self-doubt and barriers that are common to us all; yet, we have to trust and believe his words. Self-reliance can be a challenge to us all, and the quickest way to overcome this hurdle is to understand what, specifically, is holding you back. Overcoming your hold-backs will be a critical breakthrough on your *Bet on You* journey.

IDENTIFY YOUR HOLD-BACKS

Ask yourself: Why haven't you been successful *yet* at taking the first step or completing a critical milestone on the way to pursuing an important goal or passion? Is it . . .

- Timing—a.k.a., "Now's not the right time."
- Money—as in, there isn't enough?
- Someone else—you don't have the support of a critical stakeholder?

Or, is your hold-back internal:

- Your fear of mistakes and failure?
- An inability to prioritize?
- You don't have faith you can follow through?
- A past failure that has shaken your confidence?

There could be other hold-backs, too, of course. To bet on yourself, you need to understand what's holding you back. We're here to say that everything can be overcome . . . and we mean *everything*.

In the decades we've committed to supporting leaders, we've yet to meet any professional whose dreams were beyond their capabilities. Instead, we've met many who've allowed fear, worry, and insecurity to dim their ability to envision success that matters deeply to them and prevent them from taking the steps necessary to live that life.

Fear kills more dreams than failure ever will. Understanding your fears, in relation to risk, will allow you to recognize your risk disposition—your personal relationship with risk. This awareness will allow you to appreciate where you are with risk, and what you need to do to rightsize it so it doesn't prevent you from achieving what matters most.

YOUR RISK DISPOSITION

When you hear the word *risk*, what's your reaction? For the extremely risk averse, it makes them nervous—racing heart, sweaty palms. They transition quickly from an "Open for Business" mindset to one that's "Sorry, We're Closed" as thoughts of loss (and not prospective gain) race through their minds.

On the other hand, for those who skydive, swim with sharks, or even day-trade, they're likely biased by their thrill-seeking gene. The idea of risk gets their hearts racing and they're "in" before they even hear fully what type of financial/emotional/ physical risk they could be embarking on.

Your reaction to the word is important—only you know how the idea of risk can make you feel. Yet, what's more valuable to you when it comes to taking risks is that wherever you are, you can change. Risking is a learned behavior, meaning that you can redevelop a whole new relationship with it if you're not satisfied with the one you have.

It's important to know your relationship with risk is influenced by a variety of life experiences. We want to focus on the most foundational one, which stems from key figures in your life—your parents, with a particular emphasis on your mom,[8] or maternal figure. How your mom perceived, and enacted, risk had a powerful influence over you, starting from the earliest stages of your life.

In a study conducted by Friederike Gerull and Ronald Rapee, the researchers wanted to understand *if* and *how* a mom influences the fears of her children. After all, fear is the greatest risk blocker known to humankind. They designed their study by bringing in toddlers and sharing with them novel, fear-based stimuli, specifically, pictures including snakes and spiders. These images were paired with an image of their mom, with either a negative or positive facial expression. Several minutes later, the toddlers were shown the same pictures, only this time paired with a neutral expression from their mom. At the end of the study, guess what had the strongest influence over these toddlers? You've got it—seeing their mom's negative reactions.

While the results of this study shouldn't be surprising, we hope that they're illuminating. Over time, you learned what to be excited about, and what to be afraid of, simply by observing your maternal figure. So, if your mom was cautious and nervous, you learned to become risk averse; or, if your mom was more encouraging and empowered you to take risks, you began life with a higher tolerance for risk and a greater willingness to bet on yourself.

Knowing this research, suddenly a few of the bolder choices we made earlier in our lives made a lot more sense, like joining the Marines—an organization where there are 174,000 members and only about a thousand are female officers. While we've always believed that having our parents' support made this decision for us seem less intimidating, we never really considered how our moms' parenting style influenced our confidence in making this commitment. (Thanks, moms!)

Right now, as you're probably thinking and remembering all those messages you picked up in your youth that either helped or hurt you in life, know one thing: The point of this isn't to make you mom bash, or create a bunch of *would've, could've, if only* . . . statements. Besides, there's no time machine available to travel back to key moments and change your course.

We want you to value who you are and where you are, and with that knowledge know you can advance your relationship with risk by using what's available to you right now—your self-awareness and some great internal resources to tap into, your mindset being one of them.

MIND(SET) OVER MATTER

You probably don't realize this, but there's a war going on in your mind when you're either presented with a risk or contemplating taking one. Those moments where you wonder:

- Do I bring this up, again, with my spouse?
- Do I tell my boss I'm applying for the position in a different group?
- Do I accept the volunteer coaching role for my son's Y team?
- Do I speak up and present this counterpoint at our team meeting?

The war is between two coexisting and competing mindset states that are within all of us—prevention and promotion. One is telling you to play it safe, don't rock the boat; the other is telling you yes, go for it, you've got this. Your challenge isn't so much to stand back and let them go at it until one prevails—after all, we're talking about taking risks with intention, not observing a cage match. Rather, it's to be aware that these states coexist and then channel the right one for the respective occasion when it's needed.

Promotion state is focused on self-development, growth, and advancing toward what matters most to you and your goals. It's the mindset that helps you aspire to and focus on the benefits your goals can bring when you step out and into something new. It provides the motivation to stretch, reach, heighten, and sustain.

Prevention state is concerned with the safety and security side of your house and is accompanied by a thought process that emphasizes what could go wrong. Whereas promotion motivates you to go for it, prevention holds you at status quo because the fear of loss will play a bigger role in the decisions you make (more so than the anticipation of gains).

There's always a time and place for either of these mindsets to take the lead. The question always is which mindset is the right one? Often the answer comes down to your goals and the situation.

There are times when it's valuable to lead with a prevention mindset—*like when you're maxed out.* Maybe you just had a baby and started a new job; now might not be the time where you accelerate on a backyard remodeling project or take up golf. In harried times like these, you may need a prevention mindset to prevail while telling your promotion mindset to pause for a second.

Likewise, there are times when your prevention mindset needs to yield to your promotion mindset, like when you're taking on a new role at work and you're challenged to innovate. Now isn't the time to play it safe; now's the time to imagine new, test, prototype, fail fast, and apply learning going forward.

As Angie will share, in times when you're presented with

new ideas that require a promotion mindset, you need to remind yourself that it's your strengths, and not your weaknesses, that you should lean into.

RISKING IN CAREER: ANGIE'S STORY

Let Promotion Take the Lead

"If you guys want to write a book, you really need a platform. If no one knows who you are, why will people buy your books? You should start speaking on leadership to businesses, build an audience, and that will attract a publisher."

That was great advice and direct from the literary agent Courtney and I shared our first book proposal with in the early 2000s. Our proposal, which in hindsight was pretty rudimentary, caught this agent's eye because of its uniqueness—two women writing on Marine Corps leadership. But what he was conveying to us was that, if we had any hopes of selling our book, we needed to do more than write a good book. We needed to start a company to back it up.

First, the hard reality: I didn't know how to go about starting a business. I was an English major—I liked words, not numbers. Courtney and I decided, too, that if we were going to start a business, it would require that we each make an investment into the entity to get it off the ground—something to the tune of $5,000, which is no small change. I was newly married, and we'd just bought our first house. There really wasn't $5,000 I could part ways with at that point; I knew it might mean that I would have to put a portion of the upfront investment on my credit card.

Also, I was afraid. If the business started to gain traction and showed promise, I'd want to quit my job in pharmaceutical sales and dedicate my effort to Lead Star full-time. In other words, I'd walk away from a much-appreciated steady paycheck without knowing how long it would take me to replace my income. It's hard to imagine now, but I actually started resenting the fact that I had this big, bold vision for what my life could be if I took a risk, while simultaneously wishing I could just find peace and happiness in the steady, stable life I'd already built but wasn't fulfilling. Crazy, I know.

It became clear to me that I was pretty great at stoking my self-doubt and listing all the reasons why I shouldn't try something that really enticed me both emotionally and intellectually. Then one day I decided to switch the dialogue and start asking myself for reasons why I should, in fact, move forward. Unbeknownst to me at the time, I was letting my promotion mindset finally take the lead.

First things first. I knew I could write, so that aspect of the work, while daunting, I believed I could tackle. (Score one for the English major!) I was also comfortable as a public speaker, so the job wasn't intimidating. And I'd spent three years working in sales, so I had experience with business development.

I then thought of Courtney and all the skills she brought to the table. She's an attorney and knew a lot of the business start-up requirements. She also had friends in marketing and was more aware of what we needed to do to get our brand up and running.

She is also a visionary and is great at setting things in motion. I'm less of a visionary, per se, and more of a planner/executor-type person. I can work a plan like no other.

I remember valuing our joint strengths and appreciating their complementary nature; we made a great team. When Courtney and I talked to confirm that we were both in, a memorable line from that conversation was, "If not us, then who?" If we can't get this off the ground, who gets to?

IF NOT YOU, THEN WHO?

We bet on ourselves then, and continue to do so today, by fueling our ambitions with a promotion mindset and believing our strengths can help us overcome any obstacles. We often use the mantra "If not you, then who?" to motivate each other. The more success we've experienced, and the more successful people we've met, the more we realize there are no skills or super-secret sauce that divide those who prevail and those who don't. There's just a willingness to bet on yourself and take action toward what matters to you. And, when we hit a roadblock or must confront a weakness that's holding us back? We're not shy to ask for help.

On your *Bet on You* journey, you shouldn't be shy asking for help, either. Some of the initial help is actually the kind you can give yourself by tuning in to the conversation that's going on in your mind when you're contemplating inviting risk into your life and understanding what's driving the dialogue, recognizing whether it's your prevention or promotion mindset. And, then, being quite conscious of the mindset that you let dominate, ensuring it's the right one for the occasion. You might realize, through your own personal mind meld, that you're better suited for the risk you're envisioning than you've ever thought before. Just like us, ask yourself, *If not you, then who?* If you can't achieve success in this endeavor, who gets to?

HAVE CONFIDENCE, EXPERIENCE WILL FOLLOW

Your risk disposition will prepare and position you, mentally speaking, for taking on risk. These qualities, though, need a friend to help them believe that achievement is possible. That friend is none other than confidence.

We love this topic, so much so that we've developed entire full-day courses on this topic alone. What's always interesting is the intrigue around this skill, as well as the debate about its origin, especially when we ask a simple, semi-leading question in our workshops:

What comes first—experience or confidence?

In other words, does experience give you confidence to try new things, or does confidence give you experience to find new experiences? (We'll let you think on that for a second.)

What we've discovered is that in nearly every classroom the group is split. Half will make a brilliant case for why you must have experience before you build confidence. The other half will tell you that you must have confidence to even put yourself in a position to build experience.

So, what's the right answer? While we could make a great case for either viewpoint, we'll have to say we tip the scale toward the need for confidence before experience.

Experience often takes years to develop, and you can feel as if you never seem to have enough to take on whatever it is that you want to do. Confidence is an emotion, one that can be managed in an instant to give you the courage to act. You can't have one without the other. And, when it comes to taking risks, you'll need confidence to take the wheel, because you're stepping into areas where you have no firsthand experience.

Betting on yourself requires you to realize the value of you. That realization starts with believing in yourself when tested, which is the true definition of confidence. What's always interesting is when it comes to our challenges, there are times when we believe in others much more than ourselves. You need to resist this temptation to trust others to solve your challenges—you've got enough talent, capability, intellect, and drive to achieve whatever it is you've got on your mind. But it's not enough for us, or others, to believe this. You must, too.

BUILDING SELF-CONFIDENCE

Your personal confidence is built through taking risks that get you into the arena of experiences. Not uninformed, haphazard risks, but through your ability to define something you want to do and then committing to the process of doing it. If you want to run a faster 5K, for example, the simple way to describe how you'd meet that goal would be to evaluate your current time, then set a goal time, and then do the work to achieve your goal— to narrow the performance gap that exists.

Yet we know that most goals worth achieving are rarely that one dimensional. To run a faster 5K, it might not just come down to running. You might research nutrition, understanding what your body needs to perform at a better level. Or you might look up a running plan from a well-respected coach to provide the structure you need to succeed. You might share your goal with a friend to hold yourself accountable to progress.

We know that beyond the physical work you'll do to achieve your new 5K time, there will also be emotional work. You'll have to motivate yourself to prioritize your workouts and have the discipline needed to actually do what you intend. Some days you'll be excited to run. Other days you'll want to do anything but. Time and time again, your success will be determined by how well you respond to setbacks, loss of focus, or even just the busyness of life that gets in the way of your vision for success.

The commitment and commensurate actions you take toward betterment are the actual risks that help you build self-confidence. Once we tell ourselves we want to be better at something, it should be noted that, yes, we're risking failure. When we're successful, we're rewarded with increased confidence and experience. And when we don't meet our goal, we're rewarded with just as much experience and confidence, as long as we process the experience through reflection and learning:

- Why weren't we successful?
- What would it take to have been successful?
- Is the goal still so important that we're willing to risk another attempt and, of course, further failure?

As a good friend of ours shares, failure is the tuition you must pay to reach your dreams. Confidence is what gives us the ability to try again, with greater knowledge and often greater hope than we had during our initial effort.

Growing our confidence requires us to keep testing what's possible for us. It doesn't require outstanding talent or superhuman gifts. It just requires a willingness to enter the arena of life and take a chance on ourselves. To have the courage to do this, it's helpful to understand that the joy of our lives is not defined by the goals we set, but by how we embrace and experience the journey toward where we want to be. Whether we set and achieve small goals, or we go for monumental ones, our confidence expands when we successfully navigate the detours, setbacks, low points, and barriers to getting where we want to be.

The stronger your history of trying what you want to do, the more you'll build confidence. The more confidence you build, the easier betting on you becomes.

JUST ~~DO~~ TRY IT

Trying has gotten such a bum rap in our society, perhaps due to the popular Yoda phrase: "Do or do not, there is no try."

Let's face it, we're all pretty fortunate knowing the galaxy's future doesn't depend on our success or failure in the bets we want to make on ourselves. So, let's take some pressure off of us for a moment. The experiences you're acquiring to build confidence are like attempts to see where you want to place your bets. We shouldn't be afraid to try.

We've coached many people to their next level of success; rarely have we talked with leaders who regret having tried something. More often, we see professionals who keep themselves in an extended holding pattern, working to muster up the courage to take a step into what seems like the scary unknown, commonly referred to as the pursuit of their dreams.

During these holding patterns, people will share many reasons they aren't going to take a risk or try something new or different. Often, they'll cite financial reasons and how they can't risk their retirement or livelihood to switch gears. Sometimes it's a lack of talent or skill they describe as the reason they won't take a chance. Or, they might lament, "It's not about what you know; it's about who you know," as they declare their network is inadequate and there is no one to open the door to a coveted opportunity. They might even explain that any detour would look bad on their résumé, giving more power to a piece of paper (oh, yeah, by the way, a paper they write themselves) than living a life of opportunity and rich experiences.

If you ever find yourself delaying making the choice to try something that is truly on your heart for pursuit, keep this in mind:

> Trying is exactly what it takes to build
> the courage and confidence to bet on you.

Courage is not the absence of fear, it's your ability to face your fears and move forward despite of them. Through that courage, we build self-confidence on our way to becoming self-reliant and ready to embrace the moments that will define our lives. Moments and decisions that bring us joy, satisfaction, and the opportunity to contribute. And, of course, moments we look back on with pride because we listened to our own voice, believed in ourselves, and made the bets that were right for us.

RISKING FOR IMPACT: COURTNEY'S STORY

Self-Reliant in the Moments That Matter

"Trust yourself, Courtney," I whispered as I sat in my office twirling a pen between my fingers, hoping with each twist to conjure up a solution to my dilemma.

I was six months into what had begun as a surprise run for public office. After my local representative on the county Board of Supervisors passed away while in office, I was approached and asked to run for his seat. It took me many hours of personal reflection to determine if I could balance this role with my work at Lead Star, as well as determine if I really wanted to do this.

When I came to the conclusion that I was "in," I was all in—100 percent committed. After a quick primary win, I was now my party's nominee for the office.

The general election was just five weeks away, and my opponent was ramping up his negative attacks on me as we headed down the final stretch to Election Day.

In choosing to run for public office, my main goal was to add value to a very hostile, frustrating, political world. Many (including me) believed campaigns and political rhetoric had reached new, divisive lows, and that citizens were sick of the insults and mudslinging. In choosing to jump into the fray of running for local office, I had promised myself, my campaign team, and the volunteers working to get me elected, that I would run a productive, positive campaign. Instead of insults, I'd focus on the issues, ideas, and opportunities to improve our community.

My opponent, however, chose a different path. His campaign team filled mailboxes in the district with mailers that had been photoshopped to place me at events and places I hadn't been. His supporters also created a fake Facebook profile and page, trying to bait me into commenting on it in ways that would give him an opportunity to twist my words against me. Everything about his team's down-to-the-wire effort seemed to reflect the negativity, lies, and ridiculousness that were making politics unbearable for many.

My team had grown weary from the attacks. And now, my advisors were encouraging me to change the plan. Instead of focusing only on the issues, they wanted me to swing back and match his all-out negativity with my own fighting spirit. They had dug up dirt on my competitor and even went so far as to draft some equally nasty mailers I could send out to counter his rhetoric with my own insults. Everything about the proposed plan seemed wrong to me. Yet here I was in my office, twirling the pen, and considering it.

I had just hung up the phone with one of my most dedicated campaign volunteers, who was urging me to pull the trigger on the mail campaign. She had shared that she feared it was our only hope: "We have to go negative, Courtney. It's the proven way to win these close races. Now is the time!" she urged.

With reflection, I realized that going negative with my campaign was the total opposite of what I valued. I knew staying positive and trying to take the high road wasn't going to be a popular choice with my team and supporters, yet I decided I wasn't going to allow our campaign to become just like many others. I was ready to risk losing in order to stay true to the commitment I had made at the start to run a positive campaign. While this self-reliance at a pivotal moment wasn't celebrated by my colleagues, it gave me significant peace and energy to campaign with vigor during the run-up to voting.

On the night before the election, our race was forecast as too close to call. I thanked key members of the team and shared with them how much I valued their time and contributions and how, as challenging as it was, we'd worked hard to do things differently. And, no matter the result, we had much to be proud of.

I spent the entire Election Day shaking hands at the polls and thanking voters for turning out. After the polls closed, I went home to shower and change for the watch party, soon learning that our campaign seemed to be ahead. We would eventually go on to win the race by 11 percent, a margin considered to be a political landslide.

In the early dawn hours, as I fielded a congratulatory call from my U.S. senator, I reflected on the campaign. While winning felt good, what I felt best about was the choice to rely on my values when most were encouraging me to shift course. Ironically, I wouldn't last long in public office. While I had won a big victory, I found that serving as an elected official wasn't a good fit for me. I didn't value the power, status, and prestige of the role. And, I found it increasingly difficult to stay true to who I was.

Over time, I realized that my work in the private sector was a much better way for me to contribute. Eventually, I would resign my seat, having no regrets from my attempt to become more politically engaged.

I deeply value the experience and understanding that could only have come from trying. When we step toward our dreams, we don't always end up where we expect, and the gains we experience aren't always the ones we initially hoped for, but are valuable nonetheless.

If I hadn't taken this chance when the opportunity presented itself, I'd still be wondering (and daydreaming) about political life. Not only do I now know, but I'm also more aware and definitely more confident in my ability to believe and trust my own intuition.

EVERYTHING IS BETTER
WHEN YOU BET ON YOU

We all seek a life well lived. None of us want to find ourselves at the end of our life with many regrets. When you learn to bet on yourself, you will encounter challenges, mistakes, and many glory moments. Most important, you'll be living a life that matters to you. When you follow through on your dreams and desires, your worst-case scenario is the even deeper self-knowledge that you gain through missteps. With that knowledge, you enhance the power to redirect your efforts in better ways.

Betting on you is the only way to consistently find the next steps on the path toward a fulfilling life. It's how you begin any new, exciting chapter. Or how you bring who you really are more fully to the relationships you value the most. When you believe in yourself, you give yourself the best shot possible to find and maintain satisfaction throughout the journey of your days. And, like a well-toned muscle, the more you bet on you, the stronger you become. It's a great habit to build.

You have goals for a reason. When it comes to achieving them, who other than you can do this? And, while not every bet pays off, you'll never achieve lasting rewards without the courage to take a chance on yourself. After all, if not you, then who? Who is best to live the life you want? Only you.

PUTTING IT INTO PRACTICE

- Continue creating your personal Risk Manifesto at www .leadstar.us/bet-on-you, where you can explore what could be holding you back from embracing risk.
- Spend time identifying your respective strengths and opportunities for development and preferences.

- How will you save yourself? Challenge yourself to iden-tify areas where you could become more self-reliant.

- Think of a goal you've had but haven't taken steps toward. Take time to list your hold-backs and how you can over-come them.
- Become more aware of the time you spend in promotion and prevention mindsets. If prevention mindset is your default, learn to coach yourself into promotion mindset by examining risks to see why you should take them, before considering why not.
- Manage your confidence. When tested, choose to believe in yourself.
- Just try. Enjoy the journey your experiences will take you on.

DEFINING SUCCESS AND DOING THE WORK

CHAPTER THREE

DREAM IT. OWN IT. TAKE IT.

"If you want to be happy, set a goal that commands your thoughts, liberates your energy and inspires your hopes."

—ANDREW CARNEGIE

QUICK LOOK

This chapter shows you how to improve the quality of your dreams, so you can stay accountable to action and become more willing to consistently bet on yourself.

THOUGHT STARTERS

Risking well is not about dreaming bigger. Our odds for success improve when we dream better.

Building a bias for action is how you show ownership of your goals.

Don't wait for your turn—life isn't a line at the fair. Take your turn.

The guidance we've been given throughout our lives on dreams hasn't changed—*Dream Big.* Yet, our lives have changed a lot since we first heard this message.

First, the concept of dreaming—today, as adults—sounds fantastical, doesn't it? When you hear the word *dream*, doesn't it conjure up a place in your mind where unicorns and rainbows meet? A La La Land you can escape to and imagine a world that's unrealistic, unattainable, yet magical because it transports you away from reality?

Also, as adults, we just don't dream the way we did when we were young. Daydream, that is. The lulls in our lives when we could be setting our mind adrift—on the train, on a bench while our children play at the park, in a waiting room—are far-too-often filled with distractions:

- Screen time designed to help us pass the time
- Worries, doubts, and fears that consume us
- Hasty text exchanges that sort out the details and logistics of our lives

We need to dream, though. A dream is really a vision of a better life for you, a direction on where you should develop goals that make life more satisfying. Daydreaming is also a powerful tool available to help us be more creative, insightful, and to innovate solutions to challenges that we might not have considered. Research shows that when our mind wanders, different parts of our brain activate, accessing information that may have been previously dormant or out of reach. Bob Samples, in describing this process, wrote: "Albert Einstein called the intuitive or metaphoric mind a sacred gift. He added that the rational mind was a faithful servant. It is paradoxical that in the context of modern life we have begun to worship the servant and defile the divine."[1]

So much of our world today reminds us to focus and concentrate; when it comes to thinking about your future, you have to be unmoored, mentally speaking. This can help you reimagine better for you. And as you do, we think it's important to help guide you, specifically, into thinking of your context and how you can create better for you, which is why we want to share five questions to help you bring clarity to your dreams:

- What does your kaleidoscope look like?
- What's worth pursuing?
- Can you reach a starting point to your dream?
- Can you resource your dreams?
- Does the challenge seem fun?

Question 1. What does your kaleidoscope look like?

Earlier, we introduced the concept of using a kaleidoscope to help visualize where you should be directing your risks. When you imagine the chambers of a kaleidoscope to be components of a balanced life, you get a sense of not only what you value most, but of how you're engaging across these key areas or lanes of your life. Ideally, each of your chambers has the same amount of brightly colored chips, indicating that you balance your time and engagement across each of the aspects you believe are essential for a good life.

As you reflect on the four chambers you believe reflect your most important priorities for life, pay attention to the chamber or two that might not be getting enough attention from you. What are the goals, hopes, or aspirations you have for those areas of your life? Understanding what's missing from your day-to-day routine can be a great place to start dreaming better.

We often ask our coaching clients to describe their ideal day. We have them write four or five paragraphs about what that day would look like. Where it would take place, who they would share it with, what they would be doing. While we encourage them to share anything and everything they would love to do on that day, most leaders don't write about an outlandish, outrageous day spent partying on a luxury yacht in the Mediterranean.

Instead, they write about a day that most often includes being valued at work, quality time with family and friends, time in nature, and plenty of rest—days that are actually within their grasp to live fairly often. Dreaming better is about knowing what satisfies you, and taking the steps to bring those aspects of life into your days, weeks, and months. While every day won't be perfect, by using a kaleidoscope strategy to guide your actions, you can more quickly and intentionally bring balance back to your life when it gets off kilter.

Question 2. What's worth pursuing?

To dream better, it's important to have a clear understanding of what you truly value achieving. The more capable you are (and trust us, as you get good with risking, you'll realize how many talents and strengths you have) the more you need to be selective about what you set forth to accomplish. You can do pretty much anything, especially if your goals speak to both your head and heart. Yet, no one can do everything. And just because you can excel or achieve in a certain way doesn't mean it's what you should be doing.

Think of past dreams or desires you've had. Or of a time when you were successful, but upon arrival, your accomplishments didn't seem all that fulfilling or exciting. It likely wasn't that the goal was off, it was the path you took to pursue it. We've experienced this in business a time or two. Times when we've identified a goal within one of our chambers, pushed hard to achieve it, and then when we got there, it just didn't feel as grand.

Early on, when we started Lead Star, the idea of earning $1 million in annual revenue was something we set our sights on.

Less than 10 percent of all businesses achieve this mark. We believed when we passed this hurdle, we'd have made it. We both can easily recall the day when we reached the mark, it wasn't the triumphant moment we'd expected since at that point our business was full of complexity and challenges, and we were too burned out to feel good about anything. In other words, we "made it"—but it didn't feel like it. That type of success didn't seem sustainable. We met the goal but realized we needed to be much more intentional about how we were meeting it. Instead of taking all the work we could generate, we began to better understand the types of clients we worked best with, or the types of projects where we could have significant, positive impact.

Bringing our values, preferences, and past experiences to the process of understanding what type of work was of the highest, best use of our time and strengths brought us clarity. That clarity helped us focus our efforts so that future years felt not only more enjoyable and satisfying, but we were also able to help deliver stronger results for our clients, too.

As you work to determine what goals and paths to your dreams are worth pursuing, let your values, as well as any additional insight you have on you, inform your journey. If your career fills a chamber, and advancement is important to you, know that there's more than one path to get there. Or if health is important to you, know that there are thousands of ways to be healthy. Be imaginative with your route so that your journey is more enriching than the destination.

When we invest our money, we are often focused on the ROI, the return on investment, the earnings we'll receive from the choice to invest. We encourage you to bring that theory to which dreams and goals you decide are worth the effort. Time is one of the most limited resources we have. And it's nonrenewable. By reflecting on ROE, the likely return on your effort, you gain perspective on whether a hope, dream, or goal is really worth your valuable time and energy to pursue. If it's something that incorporates living the values you cherish the most, then it's worth it. However, if it provides you opportunity in just one of the chambers of your kaleidoscope, proceed with caution. Achievement after achievement in just one lane of life often doesn't equate with fulfillment.

Question 3. Can you reach a starting point to your dream?

Better dreaming not only means determining if a goal is worth pursuing, it's also helpful to understand if you have access to starting points that will launch you on the journey toward the success you imagine.

As a young kid, Courtney enjoyed learning about NASA, and she often wondered what it would be like to be an astronaut. When she was making the choice to join the military and learned that military pilots made great astronaut candidates, space travel suddenly popped up in her visions again. Then she learned that Marine Corps aviators had to have 20/20 vision, and her vision in both eyes, uncorrected, was about 20/400 since she was twelve. She realized that this path was no longer just a stretch—it wasn't possible. It was definitely a disappointment, but at least gave her insight around what was achievable in her career.

Our adult dreams can often look different from our child-hood dreams—they're more contextualized and, due to our life experience, we're more aware of the requirements for them, so we've weeded out a few that are beyond achievement. Like, for example, Angie's childhood dream of one day being Madonna. Not only was it unrealistic to be someone else, but with her danc-ing and singing (in)abilities, the likelihood for success was pretty dismal. Today, her better dream is to travel to Madonna concerts at different venues throughout the United States, something that will require intention, but is definitely within her grasp.

We want our dreams to be high, of course, but we also want them to have clear ways to progress toward them. Imagining those starting points helps you determine if the path forward will be worthwhile for you.

For example, if your degree is in finance and you've worked in accounting, it's possible to transition into supply chain if that's what interests you. You may need additional schooling, or you may have to reapply for the position at your current employer, but the path exists for you to transition. Or, if you'd like to take a downshift in your career for a year while you adjust to being a new parent, and your company doesn't present flexible offerings, there are employers that do. It takes some work to find them, and you might need to take a step back, professionally, to clip into an opportunity, but the path exists.

Timing also comes into play with reaching starting points. Perhaps you are offered a promotion that requires extensive travel, but you've recently made a commitment to care for your aging parents. When your personal priorities and choices appear to limit your access to a starting point, that's not defeat—it's just a sign that timing is really what's making the starting point difficult to access. Realizing that something you want to do isn't ideal now can inspire you to plan for it in a season when you'd have full access to the starting point.

Question 4. Can you resource your dreams?

We can all relate to having champagne dreams on a beer budget. Knowing the costs of your dreams in time, dollars, and effort is important. Don't allow a lack of resources to discourage you from following your dreams, though. Instead, incorporate imagining possible paths forward as part of your better dreaming. When you find yourself imagining all the crazy things you could do to get what you need to keep stepping toward a dream, then you know you are following up on something meaningful and valuable to you.

One of the main reasons we joined the Marines was to earn

resources for our education. Looking back, we think it's funny how student loans scared the heck out of us, but the idea of putting our lives on the line to serve our country, while earning education benefits, didn't seem too intimidating. (That also explains how much we value adventure and challenge.)

Part of dreaming better means planning a path to obtain what you need for your vision to succeed. It can be helpful to allow a goal to sit with you a bit. By playing out how you would take the first step, and the next step, and the other ten steps after starting your pursuit, you begin to envision ways to build, find, borrow, earn, or make the resources you need for your dream to become a reality. When your dreams align with your values, you'll find ways to resource them.

Question 5. Does the challenge seem fun?

We've saved the important question for last. A big part of dreaming better is about bringing greater joy and satisfaction into your life. For betting on yourself to be worth it, it's essential to design journeys that you will enjoy. That way, when the time comes for you to "Embrace the Suck"—one of our favorite Marine Corps-isms—you'll do so with the recognition that the hardship is actually something you want to endure. Besides, overcoming challenge can be one of the most satisfying things we do in life.

So, when you think about what dreams you'd like to accomplish, imagine accurately not just the glory of success, but also the pitfalls, dips in the road, and pain points along the way. When you reflect fully on the goals you have and can name and embrace the challenges you are likely to encounter, you prepare yourself not only for persevering through the tough times but also for bringing levity and even fun to trials that are found in the pursuit of meaningful success. It's a lot easier to embrace the difficulty that comes with challenge when, win or lose, succeed or fail, the endeavor you're embarking on is one that allows you to fail forward. By failing forward, we mean that, even if you miss the mark, you will at least end up somewhere good.

RISKING IN LIFE:
COURTNEY'S STORY

Mountaintop Dreams Realized and Reevaluated

I love to ski. Hands down, it's my favorite activity. Growing up on the East Coast, I learned to ski as best as I could with short runs and icy conditions. In college, my passion for the sport took me to Colorado and Utah where longer runs, fewer crowds, and powder days drew me even deeper into my love affair with the mountains. After college, before I joined the Marines, I spent a winter out West pursuing a dream to ski a hundred days in a single season. During that adventure I met my husband, Patrick. My love of skiing had led me to the love of my life.

Then, real life set in. Serving as a Marine took me all over the world, but farther from the slopes. After the Corps, building my career kept me in the office more than the outdoors. Patrick and I went skiing in the Canadian Rockies on our honeymoon, and that set the tone for skiing to become what we did on vacation during those early years of marriage and starting a family. We'd save up for an annual ski trip, investing in ski school so our kids would come to love the sport, too. It paid off, and soon our kids were leading us down the mountain.

Our lifelong love of the sport reached a pinnacle when we had the opportunity to ski in the Swiss Alps.

At the time I was working on a longer-term Lead Star project with a client in the United Kingdom, making this adventure accessible to us. So many sunny days, so much family time, and all the fresh air we could breathe inspired us all to dream better. We loved skiing so much, Patrick and I couldn't help but wonder why weren't we living in a place where we could ski as often as possible? My job was a big reason. This project would be ending soon, and we had a choice—we could go back to Richmond, Virginia, or take a risk and move to a ski town.

One night during our time in Switzerland, Patrick and I discussed how much we loved the mountain lifestyle. We also challenged ourselves to understand why we weren't yet willing to fully commit to living in a mountain town. As we shared one reason after another, laughing as we worked to one-up the other with reasons why we could absolutely not, even for a minute more, consider following our hearts, it became clear that many of the reasons that were holding us back from living our dreams were really just excuses or fears. Our kids had thrived living in Europe, even though we'd been so afraid to move them abroad. Perhaps they'd thrive again in a mountain town? We agreed to bring up the idea of moving to a ski town with them the next morning.

The next day, as we sat around the breakfast table, we shared the idea of our possible adventure with our three kids—at the time, our girls were in middle school and our son was still in elementary school. We were barely able to highlight the details before the kids loudly expressed their enthusiasm. What seemed like a huge risk to Patrick and me seemed like nothing to the kids. They were totally up for it. Clearly it was the adults who needed to build some courage (and do some expert planning).

We spent the rest of our time in Europe planning our move to the Lake Tahoe region of California. When the time came to head out, we all boldly embraced the adventure. While I had taken many risks before, this one felt like there were risks in every chamber of my kaleidoscope.

This decision led to many fantastic experiences. Living in Truckee, a quaint ski town in the Sierra Nevada mountains, proved to be magical. From cross-country skiing to mountain biking and hiking, we all grew in confidence and skill from joys of quiet, mountain living. Our children learned to navigate challenging terrain while independently seeing the benefits of following your heart to bring the adventure you want to your life.

Yet, when COVID struck, we—like so many people we knew—had to evaluate our lives and priorities yet again. We ended up making the decision to move back East to be closer to family, something we hadn't had for several years. We also knew that, as our daughters approached high school, it'd be to their benefit to live in a community that had a wider array of activities for them. This was a pretty significant change; yet, looking back, we have zero regrets.

Patrick and I know we'll head back to the mountains again in a future season. That's what dreaming better is about—knowing the constraints that are real in our lives while realizing that timing is everything and that another window of opportunity to risk will open up for us again in the future. And when it

does, we'll be quick to be both open and up for the
experience.

OWN YOUR ACTIONS

Just as dreaming is a critical component of imagining a better
life, it has to be honored by your commitment to act as if you,
and you alone, are the one responsible for it. You have to own
your dreams.

When you own something, you care for it differently than
you would if you rented it. Think about staying in a hotel overnight: When you leave the room, you likely have wet towels on
the bathroom floor, an unmade bed, and some random wrappers
spread throughout the room. If this was your home or apartment, this standard likely wouldn't fly. You'd treat it differently.

We have to think of our dreams, and their commensurate
goals, this way. They are ours, we need to own them. No one else
will care for them like we should—and why should they? Other
people have their own life, and respective goals, for themselves.
This is your life. These are your dreams and goals; therefore,
they should matter most to you.

These goals are your priorities. In life, the things that matter
to us—our priorities—don't get appointments. They're not to-dos
that can be added to our Outlook or Google calendars through
a simple invite. Our goals should always be top of mind, and
we should work on them consistently. That's how lasting change
happens; it's through the dedicated pursuit of little things that,
eventually, add up to big things.

So, once you've set your sights on a dream that matters, you've
got to take full accountability for that goal. Honor it by owning
it. Owning it means that all through the journey of betting on
yourself to achieve what you've set out to do, you are seeking

to take responsibility and resisting the urge to blame anything or anyone for any barriers, missteps, or obstacles that pop up. When challenge appears, our instinctual response can often be to look outside ourselves for reasons we aren't succeeding:

- If we're not getting callbacks on our résumé submissions, it's easy to blame the online portal or the businesses' human resources teams.
- If we're not getting accepted into a graduate program we applied to, it's easy to blame admissions.
- If we're attempting to sell our home and we're not getting offers, it's easy to blame the real estate agents.
- If we're in constant conflict with a sibling, it's easy to blame that person for his or her frustrating role in the process.

If you encounter a challenge along your *Bet on You* journey, we promise that you'll solve it when you stop looking for externalities for why you're not achieving success and start looking internally for how you can own it and act differently, you'll discover that you get a different result, and success seems so much quicker.

RISKING FOR JOY: ANGIE'S STORY

Joy Is Yours, and Yours Alone, to Own and Discover

My Marine Corps experience had a profound, lasting impact on how I live and lead my life. Not only did I acquire many great experiences during my time in uniform, but I also picked up so many incredible sayings that have served as guideposts for my actions, this one being my favorite and the one I refer to most often:

You are responsible for all you do and all you fail to do.

There's no getting around it—what happens on my watch is my responsibility. So, if I'm not happy with something, I have no choice but to own it and change it. I apply this mindset pretty intensely to my work, my physical fitness, and my family life. But if you noticed the category of this story, you might be clued into the idea that I don't do a lot to risk for joy.

I didn't realize this was an empty chamber in my life until I overheard one of my sons talking to his friend about *his mom* while I was driving them both to practice. The boys were discussing what their parents did for fun, which caught my attention because it seemed like an odd, yet interesting, topic for two ten-year-olds to discuss. I have to admit that I was curious what my son was going to say about me, so I leaned in only to hear him tell his friend, "I don't think my mom does anything but work all the time."

At first, I had to admit that I was slightly appalled at his description of me. I wanted to butt in and say, *"I do more than work! I run, I read before I go to bed every night, I make you breakfast, I take you to the beach, and I cart you around to wherever it is you want to go."* Yet, as I made my case mentally, it dawned on me that those activities either aren't really for fun or they aren't for me. I exercise to stay mentally and physically fit, read to relax, and I'm honored to make my kids their favorite meals and take them wherever they want to go, even if that has nothing to do with my enjoyment.

This was the first time I realized, in a very long time, that there was little joy in my life, and it made me, frankly, really sad that I hadn't been more intentional about having those light moments where I could smile and be immersed completely in a moment that was my flavor of fun.

After I put my boys to bed that night, I transitioned into thinking about this empty kaleidoscope chamber in my life. I took to writing about the happiest moments of my life, only to discover quite quickly that there were a few common themes—live music, theater, dinner with girlfriends, and riding my bike (not for output, but for adventure). It was apparent that risking for joy in my life wouldn't be expensive, time-consuming, or extravagant—it just had to be intentional, and I was the only one who could make it happen.

And, because I'm not a sit-around-and-wait kind of person, I owned it and started to take action. Immediately. (I think a few of my friends were surprised to get a text so late at night that read, "Let's go out on Saturday!!" My oldest son was surprised, too, but in a different way, when he woke up the next morning and learned we were going to a Green Day concert! Thank you, Green Day, for being the type of band that can bridge generations.)

One of my dearest friends, Shannon, has a great saying: "I pray like it's all on God, and act like it's all on me." I love that mentality. Now, you may not pray, but maybe you have faith, or practice offering up your dreams and goals to the world, or maybe you have sincere intentions or talk incessantly about what it is you want to do. Whatever you do to put your dreams out into the world, that's great—keep on doing it. To make things happen, though, remember that the ownership and action are yours, and yours alone, to take. Speaking of taking . . .

TAKE IT

Once you've raised the bar on how you're dreaming and understood that a bias for action and accountable ownership are key components of what allows you to leverage risk for success, it's time to understand the importance of the urgency to act, and then do so in meaningful ways.

Don't wait your turn—this isn't a line at the fair, it's not a merging lane that you're trying to zipper into with your car, and you're not ordering coffee. This is your life. It's your turn to act. Take it.

Some of the most well-known and inspiring leaders are pioneers who didn't wait to be asked to innovate. They created demand for their talent. They saw an opportunity, and they took it.

Consider J. K. Rowling: What if, at some point in writing *Harry Potter and the Sorcerer's Stone,* she gave way to self-doubt and cast her project aside? Or what if Steve Jobs, after failing at launching the home computer Lisa, hung up his inventor's hat and swore to never design another product again? Or if Sara Blakely, the creator of SPANX, after prototyping a few shapeware designs, threw up her hands in the air while exclaiming helplessly, "No woman will buy these!" and stopped pursuing her dream?

As hard as it is, don't think of these change-makers as who we know them to be . . . now. Think of them as who they were . . . then. Before they found their success. It's not too hard to imagine, is it, that these individuals all struggled to take a chance on themselves at one point? Or that once they started on their path, they questioned if they were headed in the right direction, or if their time was really best spent pursuing their dream? What would've happened if they'd stopped?

We get it: it's hard to separate these leaders from their success. It might even seem harder to relate personally to these individuals. Yet, at some point a while ago, they started out just like us—ordinary people with dreams who found the courage, conviction, confidence, and resilience to move forward despite the obstacles presented to them. They took risks, many of which paid off in very unexpected and surprising ways.

Why can't this be your story, too?

Success requires dreams, ownership, initiative, and action. Once you take action, you put yourself in a position to be better for yourself and, in turn, stronger for others. Think about all the responsibilities you have in life—to your family, to the teams and organizations you are a part of, to friends; you first must learn how to take steps to contribute and achieve. Then, once you excel at taking risks, taking chances, and owning the moments that matter, you can move toward being able to empower, serve, and support others even better.

SEEK THE HEAT

A simple way to ensure you don't get lost in your dreams and miss the opportunity of owning your future by taking action is to consistently "seek the heat" in life. By *heat*, we mean routinely putting yourself in positions that scare you . . . just a little. In these moments, don't be afraid of the heat. Besides, you're not Icarus. Your wings won't burn up when you fly too close to the sun. For mere mortals like us, heat accelerates our speed. It's a good thing.

Heat experiences are the projects, roles, or even volunteer efforts that meet any or all of these conditions—the more, the better:

- It's a first-time experience
- Results matter
- There's a chance of success or failure
- Important people are watching (sometimes it's a friend or an accountability partner)
- It is uncomfortable[2]

When we identify heat experiences that matter to us, and we have the courage to take those opportunities, growth is the reward. The more we seek the heat, the better we become at winning with risk. (And the more comfortable we become with being uncomfortable, too.) We begin to seek risk consistently; meaningful rewards consistently follow as well.

Dream better. Practice relentless accountability. And then keep shaping and taking opportunities to bet on you.

PUTTING IT INTO PRACTICE

- Examine how you can elevate and own your dreams as you continue to build your personal Risk Manifesto at www.leadstar.us/bet-on-you.
- Write down the dreams that matter to you. Use a kaleidoscope strategy to self-author goals that connect with each respective chamber and are congruent with your values.
- Practice overriding your instinct to place blame when things don't go your way. When you find yourself frustrated by externalities, turn the lens back on yourself. Challenge yourself with what you can do differently, better.

- Name your constraints. Once you identify barriers, empower yourself with the freedom to make the changes needed to overcome obstacles.

- Seek the heat—create a list of what these moments look like in your world and be intentional about discovering opportunities you can step into that help you stretch and grow.
- Don't wait for the sun, moon, and stars to align in order to take action. Build your bias for action one move at a time.

CHAPTER FOUR

CHOOSE YOUR GUIDES

"We're here for a reason. I believe a bit of the reason is to throw little torches out to lead people through the dark."

—WHOOPI GOLDBERG

QUICK LOOK

This chapter is about recognizing that successful journeys aren't completed alone, and how to identify and find the right guides at the right time.

THOUGHT STARTERS

Beyond your talent, the quality of who guides you is what ensures your risk-taking path is as efficient and inspiring as it can possibly be. Guides accelerate your success.

It's important to be selective about whom you allow to influence you. Seek credible guides who have been successful at taking risks like those you are contemplating.

Recognize that some guides are only in your life for a season or a reason. Be intentional about developing relationships with the express purpose of helping you build up your confidence and know how to take bets on yourself.

Wouldn't it be amazing if someone showed up at your doorstep one day, unannounced, and said, "Hey, I know what you want, and I'm here to show you the path you can take to get there."

We know this happens all the time in books and movies. Miss Stein, the no-nonsense book-editor character in *The Help*, did this for Eugenia "Skeeter" Phelan when she told her to "Write about what disturbs you, particularly if it bothers no one else." Skeeter did, and it led her to a career she long desired but felt challenged to break into it. Chester Copperpot, the dead scavenger, served this role in *The Goonies* as his research and historical maps led the crew to the hidden treasure that would save their parents' home.

Now, we know it's pretty clear our lives aren't carefully constructed fiction stories where the right people show up at the right time to give us the right information we can use right away. But there are people, resources, and information sites readily available to you that can serve as your guides to help venture down your risk-taking journey with greater confidence, deftness, and ease.

Eric Schmidt, the former CEO of Google, played such a role for Sheryl Sandberg, who's well known to share she was "jump adverse" when offered a job at Google in its earliest stages. At the time, she was contemplating two job offers, one with Google— the one she was excited about, though the job seemed a little vague—and another business. Eric's advice to her was, "When you're offered a seat on a rocket ship you don't ask, 'What seat?' You just get on." She followed his guidance and, well, the rest is history.

Please note that we're saying "guides," not just *a guide*. It's extremely doubtful that there will ever be a Gandalf-like wizard character who appears and sets you on your course to achieve your fullest potential. Your guides will be more of a group of people who you bring together purposefully to help support and direct you:

- An internet influencer who helps you envision an easier way to pursue your dream
- A business leader in your community who's doing what it is you want to do (and has the potential to help you)
- A fitness instructor who speaks your language and inspires you to shed self-doubt
- An author who gives you hacks and shortcuts that help you achieve . . . faster
- A coach who saves you time by pointing out potential pitfalls on your journey
- A friend who tells you the unfiltered truth from a position of love and respect
- Your boss who sees a lot of potential in you and is your true advocate

Now, most of these individuals and resources aren't served up to you on a silver platter. Your task is to find them (or recognize where they are already in your life) and be intentional with how you connect and engage with them. Beyond your talent, the quality of who guides you is what ensures your risk-taking path is as efficient and inspiring as it can possibly be. We can't overlook the importance of guides. We need them. There are very few things in life that we can achieve by going at it alone.

RISKING IN LIFE: COURTNEY'S STORY

The Rapid Learning Session

I know I'm not the only parent who imagines ways to disrupt my children's screen time by concocting "fun" activities we can do together. The air quotes are intentional. I have three kids, so what I think is fun may not be viewed that way by all of them . . . or at least, not all at once. There was one time in recent history, though, that I was sure I had picked a winner. We were going on a self-guided rafting tour.

Patrick and I had some experience rafting, so we knew what it entailed. And knowing that the trek was on a local river with only smaller, Class II rapids reassured me that we had what it took to lead our family through this voyage.

Rafting day came, and everyone suited up and got into the boat. Within minutes, Patrick and I were reminded that knowing how to do something while trying to teach our kids how to do it wasn't as easy as we anticipated. We were fine on the smooth patches of the river. Yet when the rapids picked up, our lack of skill was exposed. Before we knew it, our daughter Jessica got tossed out of the raft into a rocky patch of rushing water. Her sister Kara, a strong swimmer, jumped in to help her to safety. Both girls realized quickly the current was much stronger than it looked, and Patrick then jumped in for the rescue. Fortunately, there was a guide on another tour nearby who helped give them important, fast instruction so they could return to the raft my son and I were navigating through the rocks.

While Patrick and I never felt anyone was in immi-nent danger in the spill, we realized we'd taken a foolish risk by trying to self-guide outside our lane of experience and expertise. And the incident had clearly shaken my daughters' confidence. On the drive back home that day, I asked if they'd like to go out again soon, trying a different excursion in a few more weeks. They responded that, while they'd had a good time, it was doubtful they'd want to get back in a raft anytime soon.

Now, anyone who knows me knows I'm a leader-ship nerd, and I see leadership lessons in everything I do. Naturally, rafting through rapids is rich with lead-ership metaphors and life lessons that I could tie into. I knew that, while this rafting experience shook my daughters' confidence, without a positive experience, they might never want to attempt rafting again. So, I knew what I needed to do to bring their confidence full circle: I'd have to plan another trip.

This next time around, though, I applied some of the lessons I picked up from the experience. Now that I knew Patrick and I were not skilled enough to safely lead our crew, we sought out a rafting company that offered a guide. We needed a pro.

This second trip started off differently than the last; we had a far more thorough safety briefing than the one Patrick and I offered previously. The guide took the time to answer questions, alleviate concerns, and walked through if-then scenarios so we all knew what we needed to do if we encountered any trouble. Through all his coaching on safety, he was also fun and enthusiastic, and I could see my kids picking up on his mood. His spirit set the best tone for our trip.

We knew going into the voyage that the waters were going to be more challenging than our previous trip; there would be multiple Class V rapids. But as we were in the experience, and carefully navigating rocks, I didn't hear stress or panic; I heard laughter and saw smiling faces as everyone's confidence in their experience grew.

The second trip was longer, more challenging, and much more technical than the previous trip. Yet, with our guide, we finished this trip faster than our last and with greater skill and ease. Better yet, my kids stayed in the raft for the entire journey (I, on the other hand, was tossed out a time or two, but it only added to the adventure). When we were done, my kids begged for more.

As a parent, sure I felt a bit relieved that the mission was accomplished—a good time had by all! More important, it was a valuable reminder that when it comes to accelerating success, there's no substitute for a knowledgeable, credible guide.

GUIDES ACCELERATE SUCCESS

When we were learning how to become Marine officers, we spent a lot of time developing our navigation skills with a map and compass as we learned the fundamentals of leading a platoon in combat. We knew that one day there was potential for us to be in circumstances where a helicopter would drop us into unfamiliar territory, and we'd have to move our team from point A to point B using simple navigation tools. Sure, we could rely on GPS to help us navigate. But there might be environments where technology wasn't going to be available to us. In those situations, we'd need to be prepared to use the good ole fashioned way of moving through any terrain (woods, city streets, deserts).

We were reminded, too, that if you were to be dropped into an unfamiliar area without navigation tools, an interesting phenomenon occurs. Human nature takes over, and you often wind up walking in circles, going nowhere while wasting not only time and effort, but potentially risking your team's lives. You could say that, without a map and compass, it's similar to walking around the parking lot of a busy mall after realizing you've forgotten where you parked—disoriented and getting nowhere fast.

It's important to think about guides, a.k.a. the living, breathing version of a map and compass, in this regard, too. They are like coaches, giving us direction that allows us to be our best. As we seek to grow in our ability to place bets on ourselves and incorporate daily risk-taking into our lives, without guides we can find ourselves either really busy and not moving forward or wandering aimlessly on a path that doesn't lead us toward the destination we seek. Remember, motion does not always equal progress. Guidance from trusted leaders can ensure our efforts lead to results.

It's important for you to recognize that someone—maybe known to you or, at least, accessible to you—just might hold knowledge that is key to helping you accomplish more and enlighten and inspire you. Betting on you becomes more enjoyable, effective, and even safer when you build the right team of guides. They can even ensure that you're not wasting one of your most precious resources, your time.

As leadership coaches, we know that when clients engage us, they're looking to leverage our experiences so they can minimize mistakes and anticipate challenges, while taking the swiftest route possible to where they want to go. They know that we're seasoned leaders who have run the routes ourselves, and coached others along their paths. They bring us in to both challenge and support them. Together we work out fresh strategies that allow them to leverage their strengths, their markets, and their opportunities faster and more effectively. We believe our priority as guides is to accelerate the success of others and highlight the lessons that come from well-navigated experiences.

Now, there are a tremendous amount of resources available to help you achieve both your personal and professional goals. In fact, YouTube, Pinterest, LinkedIn and the like are wonderful, glorious portals that can educate, illuminate, and inform. Yet, a note of caution: often the information presents a lot of surface-level details that may not address you and the unique circumstances that you're in—like the clickbait-worthy claims of:

FIVE SIMPLE STEPS
TO TRANSFORM YOUR LIFE:

Step 1. Decide to change
Step 2. Make the change
Step 3. Appreciate the change
Step 4. Enact more change
Step 5. Realize your success

Believe us, if personal transformation was this easy, we'd all be doing it!

Internet fodder is also meant for consumption. While much will inform and inspire, it won't give you feedback, listen to your challenges, and provide you tailored guidance on how to advance. Only people can do that, which is why it's in your best interest to cultivate relationships so that when you need support, it's there for you.

The Credibility Factor

When you think of inviting others into your life to help you level up, we want you to be very selective about whom you're allowing to influence you. You're embracing risk-taking, which isn't a skill many are comfortable with. Hence the guidance you seek, compared to the guidance you might receive unsolicited from anyone around you, is specific and useful, and allows you to move forward. We've got some criteria that can help you choose your guides wisely.

They've Been There or Done That

Primarily, they have to be credible in the area in which you're seeking support. If you're new to a local nonprofit board you just got selected to serve on, it's best to find someone who's had board experience to help you understand how to prepare for the role and what to expect during your first meeting. Or, if you're looking to transition roles into a new company, beyond looking at online reviews (which can be both helpful *and* a place for disgruntled employees to convene and vent), try to connect with someone who's worked in the organization. If you don't know someone directly, go onto LinkedIn, evaluate the company page, and assess if you like what you see, as well as review how you might be connected to those who work there. The key is to seek out other people who have relevant experiences that can help you get the perspective you need to make informed decisions.

You can tell if someone is credible by the following criteria:

- They have experience in the activity you're interested in pursuing.
- They've had success pursuing this path.
- You respect their judgment and opinions.
- They're open to sharing insights with you.

We can't underscore enough the importance of credibility—mostly because there's a ton of people in our circles who may not have experience in the areas we're seeking to stretch but are nonetheless more than willing to give us their opinions. This is especially true when we're in the midst of a transition, or at a crossroads point, or even when we're on our way to achieving a milestone. Think about key points in your life—finishing a training program, getting married, transitioning careers, contemplating a move. Can you recall how many uninvited opinions you received? A ton, right?

Now, these people may be very well intentioned. We're sure your sister has your best interests at heart when she tells you she doesn't think it's a good idea to run for the school board. Or your friend who keeps sending you news links about investments gone bad out of her genuine concern for you. We're not saying ignore people; just be cautious with the weight you give their input. While contrary opinions from noncredible sources are something to be aware of, your goal is to continue to build your confidence in your own judgment so you can take advice like this and file it under "information." Information is just that—it's not a directive.

THE SEASON AND REASON OF GUIDES

There's always a season and reason for guides. As you work to better leverage risk for greater success, when you reflect on the dreams you have—and the kaleidoscope you've developed for yourself—take the time to do an audit of what type of help you need to advance. Sometimes the answers will be obvious—for example, you want to start a business and could really benefit from talking with an attorney on how to set up an entity for tax purposes. Other times it won't; maybe you've hit a wall and you don't know where to turn because you're not quite sure what type of support you need. These are circumstances when you might need the general guidance offered by a mentor, or mentors, who can ask really great questions to help you get unstuck.

We want to underscore that, for you, the best guide at the right time will have a talent for asking helpful questions. During times in your life when you feel uncertain about what it is you want, that's not something someone else can solve. A great guide won't tell you what you should be doing; he or she will prompt you to think about what it is you want to do and give you thoughts to help you discover for yourself the answer to that question.

The right guide will:

- Enlighten, not determine, the path for us
- Enhance, not dictate, our opinion
- Empower, not enable, us
- Inspire, not shrink, our confidence
- Challenge our thinking to help us level up, not down

Naturally, with these criteria, as you gain the gifts from your guides, your relationship over time will change. It's no different than your relationship with your parents: At one point, you depended on them for survival, then resources. Eventually your relationship evolved as you became independent of them. Someone who was once a trusted guide for you might become more of a peer or friend as you grow and develop. Or, that person might fade from your life. That's normal and to be expected as you begin new eras of success. We can recall many people who were critical guides for us at just the right time, and while they aren't in our lives today, we remain grateful for their support and wisdom.

So, the next question should be pretty obvious: Where do you find valuable guides?

The Big Three

Where you sit right now, you may not have been intentional about developing relationships with the express purpose of helping you build up the confidence and know-how to take bets on yourself. That's okay—it's never too late to start. We firmly believe that you need "The Big Three" in your life to help you gain information and inspiration on your risk-taking journey:

- Champions—People who have more insight, experience, and knowledge on a specific area than you and who are accessible
- Big Stagers—Thought leaders who share with you their knowledge and/or new ways of thinking (but you don't converse with on a one-to-one basis)
- No-Choosers—People who are mostly in your immediate circle not by choice (think family or coworkers), yet nonetheless surround you and whose guidance ranges from helpful to not helpful

Let's explore how to find, invite, or, in the case of No-Choosers, manage these people in our lives.

RISKING IN CAREER: ANGIE'S STORY

Finding and Serving Your Champions

"Who are you?" my friend John asked me one day, as I was recounting a story about an interesting meeting. John and I met in our early twenties, so he knew exactly who I was. What he was wondering, though, was how did I—a girl from the small town of Kalkaska, Michigan—land a meeting at the Pentagon the previous week with the highest-ranking officer in the U.S. Navy to provide them insight into their leadership development programming. John had also served in the Marine Corps; he knew that invitations to this level of leadership didn't happen by chance. It took an inside introduction to get a VIP pass to the Pentagon. He was impressed and his question was asked from a place of curiosity to understand how it came together.

My short answer was delivered with a smile to John. "I'm a master networker." I was joking, of course. I don't know that my networking skills are that elevated. But the detailed answer, which is more valuable to you on your journey to discover champions, is that I love people and am insanely interested in other people's stories and their success. You see, whenever I meet people, regardless of the work they do or the title they don, I have a simple approach that has been incredibly valuable to me on my journey:

- Ask more questions than I answer
- Listen and learn from their stories
- Offer support where I can

That last piece is key. A relationship is two people. For a relationship to work, it's important to realize that you might not have something immediate to offer someone, but there will be times when you can help. Always, always be willing to help where there's a need.

I haven't always initiated this level of engagement. I grew up painfully shy. My mom has always been my greatest source of encouragement and advice on how to engage those around me. When I was in high school, I landed a babysitting gig with a family in a nearby town who were extremely wealthy—we're talking generational wealth here. I mean, they wore Rolexes. The value of their watches was more than the annual salary of some of my friends' parents. After a few days working with the family, I confessed to my mom that I felt very uncomfortable talking with the parents, because our lives were very different.

My mom shared with me that if I didn't know what to say, I should ask them to talk about their lives. "Angie, people love to talk about themselves. People are puzzles—you like puzzles. Ask questions to help you figure them out." That was great advice, which I've since put to great use time and time again.

A series of open-ended questions unlocks the life journey of others, revealing their thought process in key life moments. I find I learn more about life, in general, through this form of engagement than if the conversation were flipped—others spending time learning about me and asking me questions. After all, I know about me . . . I don't know about them. That's where traditional mentoring relationships, to me, don't work to their fullest potential.

I prefer the word *champion* to *mentor,* because mentoring is often presented as a one-sided, *"Please help me!"* plea that puts the mentee in the spotlight. I like to switch it around. While I'm always looking for advice and guidance, a.k.a., "help," I put the spotlight on my champion and discover the information I need through learning about their journey. Besides, when you ask people to mentor you out of the gate, it can sometimes feel too formal for folks you're just meeting for the first time. On the other hand, if you ask people to learn about their journey, it's a casual, informal relationship—it's easy and, if there's a fit, then that's a champion relationship.

And that's exactly how I found myself in the Pentagon. I had served on a board with an amazing leader by the name of Richard V. Spencer, who would later become the Secretary of the Navy. Not only had Richard served as a Marine, but he'd had a string of business successes. As I learned about his career, I knew I would also learn from his experience. I remember asking him if he'd mind me reaching out to him from time to time with business questions. I didn't want to overwhelm him, as he's a pretty busy man, so I was careful with the questions I brought to him. Then, the inevitable situation came where his advice would be important for me, so we arranged a conversation.

Richard, to his credit, did not disappoint. He told me what I needed to hear, which wasn't precisely what I wanted to hear, but that's the value of a champion. As we were wrapping up, I thanked him profusely for everything he gave me to consider. Before we said goodbye, I offered, "Is there anything I can do to support you?"

I was happily surprised when he said, "Yes." He'd been working on helping the Navy reimagine people development and wanted to know if I'd take a meeting with the Chief of Naval Operations, the highest-ranking Navy officer in the organization—a four-star admiral—regarding trends in learning and development. I casually said "yes," though I was giddy on the inside for the opportunity to support the Navy at this level.

MAKE THE ASK

Building relationships with interesting people takes your life in surprising and enjoyable twists and turns. As you approach your journey to discover how other people's journeys can add value to yours, know that to unlock this opportunity, all you must do is one simple thing: *Make the ask.*

As you seek to identify people who have guidance and insight that can further you on your *Bet on You* journey, we know that the initial courage to ask these folks for their time can seem intimidating. We want to help lighten this for you by offering: What if someone were to approach you and say: "You've got a great story. Do you mind if we connected for fifteen to twenty minutes so I can learn from you?" Wouldn't you be honored? Wouldn't that feel flattering? Wouldn't you likely say "yes"?

That's the point we want to make. Your sincere curiosity around someone else is your way to show that you respect that person's success and value him or her. Most people would be honored to share their story with you. And if they're not? They're either too busy or not really "people persons," meaning they wouldn't make the best potential champion. If people say "no," it's not that they're rejecting you. It's not personal. So, don't let any "no" put a chill on your future requests. Continue to make the ask and build relationships so you can get the right insight and inspiration for your journey.

BIG STAGERS

Just as we need mentors in our world to access wisdom and guide us, we also need consistent sources of mind fuel and inspiration to illuminate new ways of thinking, share life hacks, and provide a steady stream of inspiration on our journey.

We need Big Stagers—people who have a platform from which

they can speak that reaches the masses—to include us, and help create community. Community is key. If you're attempting to experience something new, it's always interesting to hear from like-minded people around the world who are stretching into new areas, too. After all, people in your circle might not be leveling up like you are—they may not know how to support you. But there are others who do. Big Stagers are valuable because they spark the dialogue. And the community they build can be even better, because they bring the thought leader's messages to life.

Big Stagers who create community come in a variety of forms:

- Authors and researchers
- Internet influencers
- Keynoters
- Podcast hosts
- Media personalities
- Faith or spiritual leaders
- Artists
- Fitness instructors, lifestyle personalities, and other specialty gurus

These folks, a.k.a. the Guru Squad, need to be present in our life consistently so we can stay inspired and committed to our success. It's up to us, however, to make them present, and we do so by engaging with them through different means and mediums—subscribing to their newsletters, listening to their podcasts or audiobooks, engaging with their community socially, taking their master class, or riding with them on Peloton.

As with champions, or guides in general, we don't have just one Big Stager in our life; we have a variety for different purposes. Their ideas, when consistently present in our life, help us hold our visions for ourselves on a higher plane. Let's face it, life can be a grind. When we seek to enact change, the status quo has a powerful pull, because it's comfortable. Being reminded, routinely, that we have aspirations for ourselves that exist beyond the day-to-day can be a call to keep reaching for the better that we envision for ourselves.

LOCATE THE INTERSECTION OF WHAT'S INTERESTING AND WHAT'S VALUABLE

The best way to find the right Big Stager(s) for you is, first, to discover what's most interesting to you and what type of information can be valuable to you. At this intersection, you'll find opportunity to explore. Once you enter the gateway to Big Stagers through books and multimedia, the idea is to keep positive influences and messages that are relevant to you present in your life so your inspiration can stay high. And, the great thing about Big Stagers is that they come to you on your timeline.

Our friend Cara is the controller at a large oil and gas company. It's not atypical for her to pour ten-plus hours each day into her work; add to that the fact that she has a full family life, she doesn't have a lot of spare time. Yet, she still makes room in her schedule for her personal inspiration. When she wakes up in the morning, she no longer checks her inbox first thing—she broke that habit by listening to a guided breathing meditation with an online instructor. She fills her thirty-minute commute with both silence and an audiobook, and she has a few lifestyle influencers she follows. She takes a break during lunch to walk, which is when she has a podcast pumping through her earbuds. These routines allow her to get mind fuel she's intentionally selected each day.

She shares that before starting this inspiration practice, she had a steady stream of cable news programs filling her mind that, for her, always made her anxious and angry at someone or something. She recognized this one day after a terse exchange with a colleague early in the morning. When she went back to her office, she realized that her snappiness wasn't like her, and it definitely wasn't the person she wanted to be. She recognized the source of her angst was loud, negative news that focused on confrontation, and she knew she needed to do something about it.

By switching up her media, she's changed the game for herself. With her aspirations fueled, she had the courage to take on more responsibilities at work, set her sights higher for promotional opportunities, and instill a different tone for her team (she leads a group of 140). She's initiated a learning and development series on the books she listens to in order for her team to grow, too. She knows that the consistent presence of Big Stagers in her life has inspired her to stretch; she can also attest that introducing these folks to her colleagues has had a positive influence on her workplace.

The opportunity for all of us is to start, somewhere, and invite Big Stagers in on our terms, building habits around a steady, inspiring presence in our life to lift us up as we stay committed to the goals and aspirations we have for ourselves.

NO-CHOOSERS

The final category of people we have in our life is the No-Choosers. These are the men and women who are either predetermined for us (family) or just a part of our life. Many of them are wonderful, incredible people whose love and support are key to our happiness. Yet some of them, if we're being honest, aren't always the best for us. It's not that they're bad people; it's just that they don't encourage you or offer support as you develop and leverage risk better. This could be for a variety of reasons—they don't know how to support you, they're not excited for your growth, they're nervous for you, they're a bit jealous as they see you pursuing your goals, and/or they're concerned about what your change means for them. (As we've shared, when you stretch, those around you will undoubtedly be impacted.)

For those in your life who are curious and excited for the journey you're on, pull them close—these are your people. You'll recognize these supporters by their positivity and engagement. In chapter six, we'll share more about how to engage them, because we undoubtedly need them.

For this chapter, we want to talk about those who *don't* offer you the support and encouragement you need or would like. Our advice is not about jettisoning them. The challenging reality is that the No-Choosers in your life might include your spouse or partner (a person you've actually chosen and want to have in your life) or your brother, boss, adult child, or parent—in other words, a significant relationship that you don't want to ghost out of, you'd just like it to be better. We encourage you to recognize you have options when it comes to managing these relationships well.

First, you need to remember that confidence is an emotion; this awareness helps explain why it rises and falls with each new challenge we're up against. Our confidence is also susceptible to the court of public opinion, one that never relents. We should set a goal to be very selective who we let influence our very valuable opinion of ourselves. If it's anyone and everyone, our confidence will be on a roller coaster.

We advise you to only allow opinions from No-Choosers who've shown they sincerely have your best interest at heart. We need to filter those No-Choosers whose opinions and thoughts are valuable to us, and those whose aren't as valuable. Just because someone has proximity to you doesn't mean that person always has your best interest in mind.

Often negativity is more about the insecurity of the person sharing it than its relevancy to your life. Especially when it's delivered in a self-focused or passive-aggressive way. You can always listen and be polite, but don't internalize. Instead, filter. (Easier to say than do!)

If someone isn't supportive, or is actually more hurtful, trying to influence you negatively, don't feel compelled to act on that person's suggestions or concerns that you don't share. And be cautious not to let that person's lack of support diminish your confidence. There will never be a short supply of negativity and doubt, but that doesn't mean you have to receive it, especially from those closest to you.

We need to recognize that betting on yourself changes you, and when you change, those around you will be impacted—and some of them won't like it. For example:

- If you're being considered for promotion to a senior role at work, your current work buddies might not be so excited about you becoming the boss.
- If you choose to embark on a healthier eating plan, your family may not enjoy the idea that you're not up to going out to your old favorite restaurants.
- If you want to move, your spouse might not be open to exploring the idea, especially if he or she is fine with where you're currently living.
- If you want to invest in starting a side hustle, your partner might believe the money could be better spent on another priority.
- If you want to start teaching a fitness class on Saturday mornings, your kids might not like your absence from family time.

There's an important word we want you to consider as you approach the No-Choosers whose support you need to bet on yourself—*compromise*. We're not asking you to compromise on your dreams; rather, be open to adjusting the path it takes to get there.

RESPECT AND COMMON GROUND

We recognize that not all No-Chooser relationships can be easily and ably resolved when there's conflict. We do know, though, that empathy and respect for someone else's viewpoint can go a long way when it comes to discovering common ground among those whose support you want in order to achieve your vision and dreams. While we can't make those we care about support us on our journey, we can love them without giving them influence over our lives. And just because they are in your life, they don't have to support you. Even if they want to, many don't know how. Don't make them (or expect them) to do something they lack the ability to do.

Love what you have in common and value what you enjoy doing with that person. If you continue to progress in ways that matter to you and can build your ability to show grace and compassion for everyone in your life, you might be surprised at how detractors become supporters, or how your No-Choosers become better at understanding your needs. While you wait on the possibility that people close to you will evolve and grow, too, limit the influence they have on your very precious, valuable opinion of yourself.

PUTTING IT INTO PRACTICE

- Identify your best guides as you continue your personal Risk Manifesto at www.leadstar.us/bet-on-you.

- Spend time identifying the types of guides you'd like in your life. Be specific with how you can find and connect with them, as well as what you hope to learn from them.
- Be intentional about the information you consume. By choosing your sources, not just randomly listening to anyone about anything, you can set a more powerful and relevant agenda that's connected to the inspiration you need in your life.
- Select credible guides who've demonstrated proven performance in the aspects of risking that are relevant to you.
- The more curious you are in your relationships with guides and champions, the more you'll learn. Develop open-ended questions to better understand their journeys and how you can attain specific guidance to support you—questions like "Can you share with me where you grew up and how you were raised," and "If you were me—an xx-year-old professional seeking to do xyz—what would you do?"
- Who are the No-Choosers who add value to you? Who are the ones that you're uncertain about the type of support they offer? Be clear about whom you allow to influence your valuable opinion of yourself; also, be mindful of how you engage others who aren't in the place of supporting you.

CHAPTER FIVE

DO THE WORK

"The price of success is hard work, dedication to the job at hand, and the determination that whether we win or lose, we have applied the best of ourselves to the task at hand."

—VINCE LOMBARDI

QUICK LOOK

This chapter isn't just a reminder that you have to work hard to succeed. It's also a practical guide to help you create the capacity to do the work required to realize the benefits of the bets you make on yourself.

THOUGHT STARTERS

Saying no, and managing your time like the nonrenewable resource it is, allows you to create the margin in your schedule to explore risk with action.

Success is a result of habits built through work ethic, focus, and daily commitment to activities that allow you to progress toward the things that matter to you most.

Work your dreams to the point that you create actual opportunities to decide your future. Betting on you requires you to not "opt out" of opportunities before the choice is really yours.

Imagine walking into a fitness studio where the air temperature is set purposefully at 105 degrees. For the next ninety minutes, you're expected to move through a variety of intense stretching poses and only have one scheduled water break. When you're done with the series, your mat and your clothes will be drenched with enough sweat to fill a coffee cup to the brim.

During the series, you have an instructor sharing with you positions that you'll need to move into and hold for a set time. It could be ten seconds, it could be sixty. You're asked to not get distracted by the time passing, the heat, the person to the left or right of you, or even by your own image in the mirror in front of you. Your focus is to be in the moment as you challenge your body to stretch into greater discomfort and seek to maximize the benefit of each movement.

No one, not even the instructor, knows the level of effort you're giving during the regimen. There are no grades, you won't get a personalized review of your performance after the session. Without an expectation of an evaluation, your goal for the experience could be to just "endure" as you remind yourself with each minute passing that you're in misery and questioning why you decided to sign up for the session in the first place. You could also be looking around, seeing people in the mirror who seem to be really into the experience. You could be spending the time wondering how brainwashed someone must be to want to repeat this experience.

Or there could be another tactic you employ consciously. You know you're there, in the studio, and you've committed the time to being present. You realize there could be something to learn from the discomfort you're feeling. You remind yourself that you chose the experience to stretch yourself, so you're going to push yourself, just a little harder, in hopes that, when added up, you're better off for the experience.

For the novice or the unanointed, this entire experience, called hot yoga, seems like self-inflicted cruelty. For the practice's global following, hot yoga is their salvation. For the two of us, individuals passionate about helping you gain the courage to bet on yourself and invite daily risk-taking into your life, hot yoga is a wonderful metaphor for how each day is a choice. We can fight the experience or use it to build our risk-taking muscle one small stretch out of our comfort zone at a time.

We know there are days when you feel pressure and there's heat, and there are times when you feel like you're stuck in a room that you can't get out of, so an easy fallback strategy is to go through the motions. We also know that with the right focus, and some guidance to disrupt you from the pattern that you've found yourself in, you can discover a whole new way of existing that leads you toward growth moments, new discoveries, and adventures that bring meaning to you.

Undoubtedly, life can be challenging. Enacting personal change can be hard. But not living out your vision? Knowing that your vivid dreams are achievable, but not stretching toward them? That can be hard, too. Our challenge for you is to choose the struggle you want in your life—one of untapped potential that leads to regret or one that requires you to stretch and make incremental changes to achieve the better for you, and for others, in your world?

We know you're ready to embrace consistent risk-taking. This chapter is dedicated to helping you create the context and conditions in your world to do so.

START WITH THE GUTSY *NO*

We talked in chapter two about discovering areas in your life where you're not feeling satisfied, fulfilled, or happy, and how to put effort into backing away from the obligations that you've found yourself in so you can course correct toward better options. Ironically, often the first step of doing the work to achieve what matters to you is saying no to work that is not fully relevant or worthwhile. We know that one of the hardest things to do is to start embracing the word *no* to find the margin in your life to exercise risk—for example, when we:

- Turn down another person's request of our time
- Pass on an opportunity someone believes is "what's best for us"
- Fight the guilt someone is serving us because we don't want to do what that person wants us to do
- Choose not to do something society applauds, but doesn't speak to us

These situations can be difficult because we feel like we're letting other people down. We could do the simple thing, like negotiate with ourselves: *It's only a couple hours,* or *it's only one Saturday a month,* or *it probably won't take as much time as I think.* The reality is that minutes add up, and the more time we spend in pursuit of pleasing others is less time we spend betting on ourselves. When we say "yes" to things we don't want to be doing, we're allowing others' priorities to be more important than our own.

Saying "no" can be gutsy. Saying "no" is a risk, because it invites uncertainty into both your relationships and your schedule. Yet, when you pass on opportunities, you create margin—unoccupied white space, which can be new for you. That white space is for you and risk exploration; it's not to be squandered but should be guarded with your life. Without white space, not only will you eventually lack energy and motivation to pursue your goals, but you'll also miss out on opportunities to build hope, achieve milestones, and discover the joy found in doing things you're passionate about.

The minutes/hours/days you can claim from turning down opportunities that don't connect to your interests, values, and preferences can be reinvested into areas of your life that, over time, yield tremendous results. The concept of "overnight success" is actually built in small chunks of time over an extended period. You need to consider your "no" as your fast pass into opportunities that can truly change your life trajectory.

RISKING IN CAREER: DOLLY PARTON

Say "No" to the King and "Yes" to the Queen

One of our favorite "no" stories comes from Dolly Parton, the songwriter and original singer of the famed song "I Will Always Love You."

Dolly has shared in interviews that she knew the song was special when she released it in the early 1970s and watched it rise to the top of the charts. Shortly after its release, Elvis Presley approached Dolly to record the song, a flattering and validating proposition. Dolly was definitely interested, until she was told by his manager it was typical for Elvis to retain half of the publishing rights to any song he performed. That caused Dolly to pause. In the music business, it's well known that the songwriter—not the singer—is the one who often benefits greatest from a hit. And Elvis's song would definitely be a hit. Yet, his success with her music would require her to forfeit something she valued greatly—her ownership of the song she created.

Dolly turned down the request. She told the King "no," passing up an opportunity to earn a lot of money.

But she knew there was something more valuable than cash—her integrity, her vision for herself, her standards, and her own personal expectations. What's more, and what makes this move so gutsy, Dolly made this decision without any knowledge that nearly twenty years later, a movie called *The Bodyguard* would come around, Whitney Houston would record the song (and not ask for any rights), and her version would smash Billboard's records. Dolly would later say that Whitney's success with her music "made (her) enough money to buy Graceland."[1]

Dolly's bold move is a powerful reminder that your "no" doesn't close doors—it may even create opportunities that you can't foresee in the moment. When it comes to right now, your gutsy "no" can set into motion many great risk-taking adventures. For example:

- Registering for your first round of online classes that sets you on your course to earn the degree you've wanted to pursue
- Going the extra mile on that important presentation at work, showcasing your talent to senior leaders
- Raising the bar on quality on a big project you're responsible for
- Creating a blog or life hack site (or any other social media presence you'd like to dabble in)
- Exploring a side hustle that could blossom into a thriving business

Your margins are important. Remember how we were taught in grade school that we weren't supposed to write in the margins? We're here to reimagine how they're used.

WORK IN YOUR MARGIN

Your margin is your time and space to do the work that helps you transition toward the better you that *you* envision. It could be an hour each day; it could be three hours each week. It's the time where you experiment with risk-taking. Remember our promise that we don't want you to quit your job to change your entire life? Your margin is your place to start your research and experimentation on whatever it is you'd like to transition into. You can use this time to network, build your LinkedIn profile, recreate your résumé, prepare and cook healthier meals, practice the guitar, or learn a new language.

Ideally, use your margin during the time of day that is the magic time for you and your brain. The time when you feel least encumbered by life's responsibilities. For both of us, our magic time is first thing in the morning. We're early risers and have found that the most productive times in our day can be found in our home offices when everyone else in our house is sleeping and we're able to focus on the more strategic aspects of our work (like creating content, writing, or imagining new initiatives) without the distraction of inbound emails, texts, or phone calls. We worked our margin when we were writing the proposal for our first book; we still had steady employment during this time, so our margin was the only time we could commit to writing. There were definitely a few Saturdays thrown in there, too, as well as many evening calls when we collaborated twenty minutes here, thirty minutes there. Many people say they don't have time to pursue their aspirations. Our argument is that you find the time for the things that matter.

For you, that time could be in the evenings. It could be when your kids are watching Disney+ and you can steal away for an hour. Or, when your partner is working late or participating in a community event. You know you—when you're least distracted, when you're most productive. Use those moments to do the work of betting on yourself.

RISKING IN LIFE: ANGIE'S STORY

Grounded and Centered

When COVID hit, my life—as I knew it—ground nearly to a halt. I was used to traveling seven-plus days each month. Now, like other business travelers, I was home for an unforeseeable future. Business, as I knew it, would also be forever changed. Our business had been a mix of coaching, keynoting, on-site consulting, and live workshop events. Now, a significant portion of our business vanished, as did the revenue that went along with it. The shock was both depressing and disorienting, pushing me into a healthy denial for a few weeks. (We'll talk about grief in chapter eight.)

I remember talking to a champion of mine at the beginning of the pandemic, the former chairman of the Joint Chiefs of Staff, General Joseph Dunford. He'd agreed to be a guest at one of Lead Star's free, open-enrollment webinars to share guidance with our audience on how to lead through uncertainty. In the greenroom before we went live, he asked how I was doing. I was pretty honest with my emotions and said I could hang in there for the next few months. He said, directly, that I needed to prepare for this experience to last eighteen to twenty-four months. I may have smiled and nodded to him when he shared that, but on the inside I felt gutted. I didn't want to believe him, but I knew he knew the realities of our situation better than anyone—the media, the politicians, business leaders—and I needed to listen to what I was hearing and adjust my expectations quickly.

Now, some people like to process their thinking by talking, or doodling, or walking. For me, I write. I find that writing brings me both clarity and direction. Later that night, I sat down to write out what I'd just heard and what, specifically, that meant for my life. I knew that I was entering a period of massive redefinition, not just professionally, and I knew I had a choice—the next two years could be among the most difficult of my life, or they could be the most transformative.

I'd always been interested in the idea of a strong mind-body-soul connection; yet, I hadn't always been a committed practitioner to focusing on each of these respective areas. I believed, though, that if I committed margin in my life—at least ninety minutes each day—to my emotional and physical well-being, as well as the consistent expression of my values, I'd have strength and endurance during COVID times for myself and others, and when we went back to "normal," I'd be better in ways I couldn't anticipate (or measure, for that matter).

In other words, in my margin I did my work on me. It felt both very selfish and necessary to guard that time, and I'm sure it was pretty frustrating and annoying to others, because they were used to accessing Angie-on-demand. But I knew my life was changing, and I could either be a passenger in the process or I could direct it. To do the latter, I needed to do the work. Direction doesn't reveal itself in one brain-storming session; it takes time and thought in order to be revealed.

I'm fortunate I made this commitment, too. During COVID, despite all the challenges, losses, and financial hits and bruises, each day I recommitted to leading my life during my margin time. This daily practice gave me time to process my world, focus on my future, and create and innovate in ways that were necessary for the period we were in. I even had, surprisingly, more time to think about how I could use what I had to help others. Having worked so much with human resource teams, the value I had to others was knowing how to write a pretty good résumé and connections to job opportunities. It was both an honor and privilege to help my friends and family members update their résumés so they could transition to more stable work; it was also great to make key introductions between talented individuals and employment. This process was invigorating and gave me what I'd seen lost in so many—hope. I worked, too, to extend this quality to others.

My firm belief is that the number one, most important leadership relationship you have is with yourself. If you can't take care of you, you can't do the things that will allow you to enter the arena where you can influence, inspire, make bets on yourself, as well as support others on their journey. The strength of your leadership starts from within. It's really that simple, but it's not easy. For many, it seems counterintuitive that to serve others, you have to invest in you, first. But you can never give what you don't have.

You deserve to show up in your life in a way that

you're inspired and amazed by what you can do, which takes time. Carving out your margin and doing the work in it are essential to your growth and development. And when you do make the time . . .

DON'T HALF-ASS IT, EITHER

Yeah. The aforementioned point is really important. If you take the time and effort to create margin in your life to experiment with new ideas and initiatives, you want to determine in that sacred space the validity of your options, if the idea is worthy of pursuing to a greater extent.

When you half-ass your experimentations, you risk making invalid conclusions about the viability of an option. It's like taking a few piano lessons, not practicing, and then concluding that you're never going to be able to play that Billy Joel song you want to play. So, you quit. The reality, though, is that you've got potential to play many songs within the Billy Joel catalog, but never gave the attempt your best effort or full focus.

Here are other ways things get half-assed in life:

- Making the decision that you're going to bring new team-building activities to your group at work and then hastily, thoughtlessly, throwing one such activity together. After it's met with lukewarm reception, you conclude that your team just isn't interested in building relationships. (Before you draw this conclusion, you should try engaging your team, see what they want to do, then build an event around their interests and preferences.)
- Submitting your résumé to a few online portals and not getting callbacks, and then determining that the jobs

you're seeking are beyond your reach. (If you really wanted to pursue a new opportunity, you'd find multiple paths to get your résumé in the door and you'd definitely follow up with a phone call to confirm receipt.)

- Deciding you're committed to improving your relationship with someone, and yet, when you're with that person, you spend time on your phone instead. (It can be hard to be here now, yet it's often the first step in strengthening our connection with others.)
- Not studying for your real estate license test and, consequently, failing it and using that as evidence that you weren't meant for that type of work. (This one is obvious—no one has ever regretted preparing too hard for test day.)

Bottom line: Half-assed efforts don't just get you poor results, you run the risk of getting false results. You can even discover that you miss out on the richness of what you were seeking from the risk you wanted to take.

Wanting something in life is never enough. Showing up is important, but it's not everything. You have to do the work to determine if a course is really for you. This requires commitment, patience, and perseverance, because the results you're seeking are never going to be immediate.

It's a common preamble for those starting fitness programs that it takes four weeks for you to begin to see the results of your efforts, eight weeks for your friends and family to notice, and twelve weeks for everyone else to see a change. In other words, noticeable results take more time than you think. While this guidance is offered for fitness, it also rings true for any other personal change.

Our hope for you is that when you commit to creating margin, you use it for its purpose—to do the work. Your risk-taking in these moments needs to be a priority. It's not the time when you squeeze in the extra stuff you need to do—like respond to emails or fold laundry. Your margin is where you execute.

After all, until you execute, it's just an idea. Doing the work makes what you're seeking a possibility and option. You can't just plan—you must do. There's a balance between planning and doing, so let's talk about that, too.

HIT REVERSE TO CHARGE AHEAD

Creating plans for anything can be really exciting. When ideas are met with description, timelines, or even vision boards, suddenly they seem to take on a whole new spirit of their own. We can't tell you how many times we've sat down with management teams to help them create both visions and strategies for their business units, and then, when everyone sees the same potential for their group and buys into a direction? Well, let's just say the enthusiasm and excitement that ensue can light up a city.

Planning can be invigorating; it's also necessary. Whenever you attempt any change, even if it's something like leading a new initiative at work, you need to put thoughtful consideration into how you're going to proceed—what team members do you want to include in meetings, what resources are available, and how are you going to deal with the challenges you can anticipate now that will inevitably pop up? Absent a plan, it's too easy to fall back into old routines and abandon all your good intentions for change.

When you go about planning, a useful tactic is to reverse plan. This means that you start by thinking about the goal(s) you want to achieve, visualize it, and give it a due date:

• I want to pay off all my credit card debt in two years.

- I want to land three new accounts by the end of next quarter.
- I want to leave the city and move to the suburbs in eight months.
- I want to know in twelve months what franchise to invest in and if it's a possible option for supporting my family.
- I want to take a biking vacation in Europe in six months.

Then, rather than create a timeline from now until your due date, start from the goal accomplishment date and create a reverse timeline. For example, what will you be doing the day before goal day? What about two weeks prior?

It's interesting that a forward plan and a reverse plan often don't look that different in regard to milestones and goal markers along the way. What is different, though, is when you reverse plan, you're better able to envision success and accomplishment, which translates into greater motivation and commitment for achievement. Research has shown it also influences the bar you set (reverse planning actually inspires you to set your bar a little higher, because through the planning process you realize you can achieve more) and the likelihood of a positive outcome.[2] When you bet on you, we want you to increase your chances for success. How you plan really matters.

So, by all means, plan—but a note of caution: Don't overplan.

SET THE 1/3–2/3 RULE INTO MOTION

We learned in the Marines that a good rule of thumb is to follow the 1/3–2/3 rule when planning. That is, one-third of your time should be spent planning; two-thirds should be spent making things happen. If you spend too much time planning, you spend too much time in a vacuum. This lost time is time you could've used to coordinate actions with other stakeholders, rehearse movements to ensure people are in sync, and discover where your strengths are and where you could be exposed. You also run the risk of losing momentum and not being ready when the time comes to take action.

Too much time planning also means that the things you want to do might not ever happen. Business schools are full of student-created business plans that are packed with amazing entrepreneurial visions that could, possibly, change the world. But they're just plans, kept on hard drives, and basically DOA—dead on arrival. Sure, they're bolstered by spreadsheets that show profitability and words that paint glorious pictures of success. But nothing works unless the work gets done.

If you find that you've got a tendency to go into overplan mode and continuously work to perfect your plan before you take action, let that be a warning that you might be avoiding risk. First, there's no such thing as a perfect plan; you're trying to perfect something that can never be perfected. We also were taught in the Marines that a plan is a reference point for change, so even if you concoct this amazingly detailed plan, the likelihood that events will unfold as you envision is impossible. There will be friction that you don't foresee, and chance happenings and surprises are just that . . . nothing you can anticipate or prepare for, but inevitably will show up. If you've ever planned the perfect vacation, and then either your partner got sick or it rained the whole time, then you get what we're saying.

As you create your reverse plan, you'll notice that there are many to-do items on your list of things to get done on your experimentation journey. To help you prioritize what should be tackled first, we'll offer that it's always best to get the tough stuff out of the way.

START WITH THE BIG HILLS

Whenever you embark on something new that's ripe for experimentation, our guidance is start with what seems the most challenging, seemingly insurmountable, task. It's also likely the most time-consuming activity. Your ability to dig into the hard stuff will determine so much, like if it's an activity you enjoy and want to be a part of and if the stretch is worth the struggle for you. You'll learn to appreciate how much time and effort you'll need to give other related tasks that you've got no experience engaging in. So, prioritize the work that intimidates you the most, first.

Say, for example, you get asked to lead a fundraising effort at your child's school. If fundraising is something you've always wanted to attempt, use your margin to determine if you're capable of achieving what's being asked of you before you commit or pass. The hardest part of fundraising is, of course, asking for and collecting money. Give yourself a day or two to call others who'd be natural donors and assess your comfort in the ask and their willingness to support your effort. Making these asks is a far better use of your time than calling others to hear their opinions of whether you should or shouldn't take this opportunity. (You can do that, too, but not before you put effort into the hard stuff.)

Or, if you want to open a microbrewery in your hometown, before creating recipes, designing a logo, and finding hops suppliers, invest time in looking at real estate to understand what rent could cost and see what type of licensing you'll need to get your dream off the ground. One trend we've noticed far too often is that aspiring entrepreneurs get caught up in the fun stuff—business branding, websites—making them late to discover that they get set back when it's time to engage in activities that will ultimately allow them to succeed—like business development, cash flow management. Cold calls and QuickBooks aren't as much fun as the expression of an idea. Yet, they're necessary for viability purposes.

Your success at the hard stuff will create confidence within you that will help you determine if you can achieve in this arena, or if the opportunity really isn't for you. What you're essentially doing by engaging in the hard stuff activities is creating choice points that allow you to move forward or give them a pass.

TAKE OPPORTUNITIES TO CHOICE POINTS

Ultimately, making opportunities real is not just about planning and preparing, it's about action. When the action involves just you and your initiative, you have more control over outcomes and effort. It gets a little trickier when whether you succeed or fail depends on external factors like bosses, markets, or gatekeepers.

We can appreciate that with many of our goals, our success is not fully up to us. Perhaps there's another person who makes a decision that impacts our progress, like a hiring manager who decides to whom to extend a job offer, or an admissions committee that determines who is best to admit to a program. It might be a loan officer who determines if a mortgage will be granted to you. External constraints can often drive leaders to rely too much on imagination and prediction by anticipating the rejection or refusal of others, instead of physically taking the steps to make it to real-life choice points.

A big part of doing the work to bet on yourself is to create actual opportunities. When the goals you want to meet rely on external factors going your way, it's important to keep pursuing them fully until you actually have a choice to consider. If you've ever found yourself thinking:

- I'd like to apply for that program, but I doubt I'd be accepted, so I won't try.
- I know I could add value to that project, but I don't think

my boss will allow me to travel during our busy season, so I won't ask to be a part of that team.
- I'd love to work internationally, but it's impossible to get visas.

What you're doing is actually failing to take something to a choice point. You're opting out before you even have an actual option. We say, put in the application, make the ask of your boss, or apply for that visa. If you're serious about an endeavor, take it all the way to a choice point instead of mentally opting out because you're afraid, unwilling, or intimidated by the ask, the process, or the risk.

You can always decide you don't want to do something. But don't discount it before it's an actual option. Rich learning and growth happen in the pursuit of choice points. Over time, success comes from what you attempt to do, rather than what you imagine you could do, but don't try. When you follow through on the work needed to turn your dreams into actual opportunities, you gain valuable wisdom and perspective.

RISKING IN CAREER: COURTNEY'S STORY

The Season of Opportunity and Serious Consideration

Like many professionals, I've had a variety of times where I wasn't sure what the next chapter in my career should be. In the midst of a particularly memorable season of confusion as to which path was best, I found myself exploring three very different options. Since I was about to graduate from law school at the time, I was interested in working for a large law firm. (Well, that might not be entirely true. I was for sure interested in the large paycheck that came with working in a large law firm, but I wasn't sure the idea of billing thousands of hours a year, often working solo in a quiet downtown office, was for me.)

In the post-9/11 era, I also found myself drawn to a national security career. Having served as a Marine, I found the idea of applying to the Central Intelligence Agency to join the famed Directorate of Operations (the small division of the Agency that handles espionage) intriguing and exciting. Being a part of the CIA definitely appealed to my love of challenge and adventure.

Angie and I were also in the process of trying to write our first book, and we were contemplating starting a company to pursue our passion of sharing leadership lessons with professionals.

While I wasn't sure which career path would be the right fit, I knew that working toward getting to actual choice points was going to be a competitive process. Dreaming about what I wanted to do was much different than getting an actual job offer from a law firm, making it through the CIA's selection process, or inspiring a publisher to put our book into print and finding the resources to start a small business. I knew I had a bunch of work to do to see, realistically, what my options were.

On the law firm front, that meant performing well as a summer associate. For the CIA, it meant navigating through months of a long process that had me self-tutoring on international affairs so that I could speak intelligently on matters around the globe, and completing an interview process that included academic testing, a psych evaluation, and a full lifestyle polygraph test. On the entrepreneurial path, this meant many planning and writing sessions with Angie as we worked to write a book proposal and find an agent to market our book.

I was certainly busy doing my best to follow up on my hopes and ambitions. And while it was an intense season for me, the rigor of what I was doing brought magic to the decision process. In weathering the fog of the journey, things became clearer. I went from dreaming to doing, and that made all the difference in creating options and making choices. By experiencing each path, I got new insight.

While I enjoyed my colleagues at the law firm, I found out quickly that even while the summer salary was great, as I suspected, the work didn't speak to me. I turned down the offer of a permanent position at the firm. Making the cut for the CIA was exhilarating. I was honored and humbled to be given a job offer. My challenge-junkie side so wanted to write future chapters of adventure like the ones I experienced in the military. Yet, I wasn't certain that the lifestyle was the one I wanted as a permanent career, because I knew, one day, I might want a family. It just didn't seem conducive to how I envisioned that chapter of my life. So, I deferred the offer to think things through before finally deciding it wasn't a fit.

Ultimately, as you can probably guess, I chose to start Lead Star with Angie and write what would become the first of multiple books. It was a path that allowed me to bet on myself. I never would have had the courage and confidence to pursue my true passions if I hadn't done the work to follow up on my other dreams. Getting offers from the law firm and the Agency affirmed that I likely had some marketable skills to use in pursuing what I wanted to try but was scared to do. Also, following through with the summer internship and the lengthy CIA interview process allowed me to gain additional awareness into what those careers would have been like and gave me the opportunity to meet people filling the roles I was exploring. Going through that hands-on discovery saved me from many "should've, could've, would've" moments, especially during the tougher moments of building a business.

If you have a goal that aligns with your values, pursue it to the point where you have a bona fide choice to make, or to a point where you can go no further. Not only does that set you up for fewer regrets in hindsight, it also provides you with the enriching experiences that give you better insight into who you are and what you really want out of life.

ORBIT THE EXPERIENCE

You can save a lot of effort and energy if you can come to a choice point and orbit the experience before you decide to move forward or back off a decision. When we say "orbit the experience," what we mean is, once you are at a true choice point, walk fully around the decision, mentally speaking, to evaluate if it's right for you:

- Is it aligned with your values?
- Is it worth the effort?

- Is this what you want to be doing with your time, with your life?
- Are these the people with whom you want to be engaging?
- Is there learning that will benefit you on your life's journey?

Sometimes, that answer is "yes." Sometimes that answer is "no." But to get there, you've got to passionately detach yourself from the choice so you can make a reasoned decision about moving forward. Our best decisions are both emotional and logical. We need emotion—it provides the motivation to succeed, and it connects to what's in our heart. Our emotions let us fall in love with what we're pursuing, making the effort worth the while. We need logic, too—it connects to our brain, the rational part of our being. We need logic to help bring wisdom and common sense to our pursuits. And, while it takes work to chart an informed course, it's invaluable effort that allows you to determine if the risks you're willing to take are the right ones at the right time.

PUTTING IT INTO PRACTICE

- Plan how you'll do the work that matters as you prepare your Risk Manifesto at www.leadstar.us/bet-on-you.
- A significant factor in your success with risk is your willingness to be creative and do the work of living out your goals and values.
- Recognize that time is a nonrenewable resource that must be intentionally leveraged and managed. Say no to distractions and activities that don't further your goals.
- A responsible way to explore risk is to use time in the margin of your life for testing, trying, and working your plans.
- Understand what time of day you are most creative,

productive, and alert. Give some of these golden hours to projects where you bet on yourself.

- Select few priorities to do well. Half-assed effort produces false results.
- Reverse plan with clear objectives and timelines.
- Remember that while planning is valuable, action is essential.
- Identify the hard parts of any goal you'd like to achieve. Focus on the hard stuff first, this will give you clarity and momentum.
- Don't opt out mentally, follow through on your dreams to actual choice points. The journey will create tangible opportunities and allow you to develop perspective on the decision.

STAYING SAFE AND RECOGNIZING WINS

CHAPTER SIX

WEAVE YOUR SAFETY NET

"Safety doesn't happen by accident."

—AUTHOR UNKNOWN

QUICK LOOK

This chapter highlights the elements of a strong safety net that will be invaluable to you on your risk-taking journey. These key elements include: your finances, your talents, and your judgment.

THOUGHT STARTERS

We do brave things when we feel safe.

Building a secure foundation allows you to bring more risk into your life.

That way, no matter the outcome of the chances you take, you'll still be better off for the experience.

Planning for safety requires balance. Don't underrepresent or overexaggerate what you need for security. Identify what *just enough* looks like for you.

We do brave things when we feel safe.

We'll rock-climb with just a harness and a belay. We'll bungee-jump, parasail, scuba dive, and skydive. We may, just may, even drive ten miles an hour over the speed limit. (Daring, we know.) And this is just in regard to our physical safety.

When we feel psychologically safe, we'll share our opinion directly, with tact. We'll feel comfortable to let our guard down and express ourselves authentically. When we feel financially secure, we might spend a little more money on a vacation, or even buy that hot-ticket item that we were hesitant to just months ago.

We can experience safety in so many aspects of our life; we know the comforting feeling. It inspires the courage and confidence to take risks because we know if anything happens, we've got measures in place to take care of us so if we trip up, we've got our own back.

We want you to feel secure in your *Bet on You* journey with the risks you're contemplating so you can do the even braver, more important things you've dreamed about doing. We don't want you taking reckless risks that, if they go bad, you're worse off than where you started. We want you taking risks that, if there's a misstep or fumble, you can rebound well and are better off because of the experience. The more experience you gain in life, the more you learn. And the more you understand which risks are worthwhile—even essential—for you to take, the smoother and more enjoyable your path to success becomes. A well-woven safety net gives you the confidence to keep stepping toward risks that matter, rather than be fearful of new or different opportunities.

We're going to help you reimagine your safety net; the elements that can catch you if you fall, so you don't fall behind. And, just as we advocate a kaleidoscope approach to imagining a life well lived, this same sense of balance is helpful when determining what can bring you the stability and security to pursue intentional risk. The three key elements you can weave together to create a stable foundation are: your finances, your talents, and your judgment.

These elements are interdependent—you need all of them, and you need to build them with diligence:

Finances + Talent – Judgment = Squandered Opportunities

Talent + Judgment – Finances = Underresourced Opportunities

Finance + Judgment – Talent = Limited Opportunities

As you examine these elements, we want to share new perspectives with you on each one. Our goal is that you recognize how your need for security with any of them is either helping you or holding you back. And, like all the risk-taking skills we've shared, these elements are areas we can develop throughout our life so as we grow with risk, our safety net strengthens, too.

YOUR FINANCES—WHAT'S YOUR NUMBER?

This isn't a book on financial planning. We'll leave that advice to the money gurus, but we'd be remiss if we didn't address this topic because there's likely a financial implication related to the bets you want to make on yourself. You might need to . . .

- Borrow money
- Spend money
- Save more
- Earn less (or stop earning for a period)
- Go on a budget
- Make a move to increase your FEP (future earning potential)

As entrepreneurs, we've got to admit that we think about money differently than a lot of people. It wasn't always this way, but when you enter the arena where your income is a direct result of your ideas and effort, you tend to see money as a renewable resource. And it undoubtedly is. Yet, it's not commonly considered that way.

Money, to many who find themselves in the position of taking risks, is a scarcity item. Because they view money this way, there never seems to be enough of it. It can be easy to buy into a belief that you need more and more to be safe or ready for risk. Or, you might believe that all you have right now is all you're going to have and, if you make any wrong moves, it'll vanish without the hope of being replaced.

Case in point, our friend Lila. When she was contemplating transitioning careers to increase her FEP, she confessed that she had an easier time imagining herself as a drug addict living on the streets of Chicago than doubling her salary in a three-year period.

Or our client, Mike, who wanted to stay in his industry but move to consulting so he could have greater flexibility. When we pressed him on what his hold-backs were, he shared that he was afraid he'd be homeless in six months if he made the attempt. (By the way, in an earlier conversation, he stated that in addition to his fully funded retirement account, he had two years' worth of living expenses in his savings account.) Mike's timeline to financial ruin clearly didn't make sense. Mike was overrelying on financial security to the point that his exaggerated need for it was preventing him from greater satisfaction in life.

It's never surprising, but always amazing, to hear people catastrophize the downside of a risk they're exploring, while giving little imagination to the great potential for upside that could result from their choices.

Money will always be a factor when it comes to placing bets on ourselves; it's a pretty important component in our overall sense of security. We can't get around it. We need money to live and, one day, we'll need our savings to retire. If where you sit right now, you think you can't afford to take a risk, then that indicates you need to expand your money knowledge and get intimate with your personal finances. If you determine quickly that your financial situation seems unstable at this time, get to the root cause and understand why. This will help you put a plan in place to shore up the resources needed to get to the position where you can take the bets on you that you want to take.

But . . . and this is a pretty big *but* . . .

For many leaders we connect with, having enough money isn't typically the problem. We've met both real and paper millionaires who were scared to bet on themselves. Despite their account balances, they've always felt financially vulnerable, which contributed to their hesitancy to invest in themselves. The key word there is *invest*.

Most view money as the vehicle to consuming and provision; they don't see it as a medium they can use to invest in their joy and contentment, their overall quality of life. We often don't think of the money that we spend on ourselves as investments, but when it comes to taking risks, money dedicated to enriching your life in ways that further your dreams and goals certainly is.

We want to be clear: We're not talking about buying a designer bag to up your Instagram image game or purchasing an expensive watch to impress your boss at work. We know we could make the argument that these are investments. For the point of this chapter, we're talking about experiences, like investing in your education so you can enter a new level of earning potential, or getting a loan to invest in commercial property, or spending money on a pilot's license, or taking a one-month leave of absence from work to attend cooking school in Italy.

The experiences you invest in come with skills, awareness, and lessons that you'll use far into the future, giving them both real and intrinsic value to you. This is the classic short-term loss, long-term gain analogy.

This is a logical way to look at our financial resources, but we want to prevent the trap that we see far too many people fall into, one in which they're so beholden to their finances that their resources are creating a barrier between them and the life they desire. Don't buy too far into a need for security to the point you deny yourself a richer life.

We have a friend, Collin, who works in a smaller, regional company that he's long believed is going to be sold one day. When that happens, he thinks he'll get about a $50,000 payout—that's no small sum. The challenge, though, is that Collin's been wanting to move to Phoenix for the past several years. He keeps delaying his dream as he waits on the business's sale—something he has zero control over. Collin has a hard time seeing both the opportunity cost of staying at the company (he's missing out on his Arizona lifestyle and the promotion opportunities as part of a bigger organization) and the reality that the payout, after taxes, may not feel like the windfall that he hopes. Believe us, we've talked with him about the possibility that he's being held hostage by a mirage. But Collin is like many other people we know in similar situations—they want one more piece of financial security before they pull the plug. The trouble is, though, that there's always one more piece.

The challenge with finances is that we need them to serve as our safety net, but there comes a time when our resources may not be serving our whole-life needs.

The key research on this topic comes from a study published in 2010 by Daniel Kahneman and Angus Deaton on the impact of income on subjective well-being, with a focus on these two factors:

- Our emotional well-being—the quality of our everyday experience, like our happiness and satisfaction

- Life evaluation—how we feel we rank in life, compared to others

Their predominant finding was that more money can buy satisfaction, but only affects our happiness up to an annual income of around $75,000.[1]

In other words, the relentless pursuit of more money may feel like we're winning the battle against those fictitious Joneses, but it could also be detracting from the quality of life we're seeking to gain with risks we'd value exploring.

Our rule of thumb is that you always need to know what you need, financially, to take risks:

- What your annual expenses are
- What your monthly budget is
- What number you need to have in the bank to feel comfortable exploring risks
- What's your rainy-day fund—the number you need to absorb any short-term financial surprise
- What your earnings goals are

We only have so many years to work and bear fruit from our efforts. We also only have so many years to take risks and realize the benefits of our choices. It's a delicate balance, and one that is not all about how much you save, it's also about putting yourself in a position for a financial upside. Risking for your FEP can be as valuable as saving for security. Clarify what you need to feel secure financially—don't underrepresent or overexaggerate this number. Discover what *just enough* looks like for you. This awareness will help you balance both your financial resources and your desire to enact risk thoughtfully, methodically.

YOUR TALENTS—STRENGTHENING YOUR ABILITIES AND CAPABILITIES

Your finances are just one aspect of weaving a safety net that gives you the confidence to invite risk intentionally into your life. Yet, contrary to popular belief, your financial resources aren't the most important component of a well-woven safety net. Angie had to experience the devastation of divorce to realize what could really bring security in her unsecure world: her talents.

RISKING IN CAREER AND LIFE: ANGIE'S STORY

You Control Your Talent

The year 2019 was challenging for me. As I moved through my divorce, I also assumed a host of new, unwanted identities—single mom, divorcee. The process itself was also overwhelming, unpredictable, and raw. I remember ringing the New Year in on the West Coast, vowing that 2020 was going to be my year. (I know, I know.) Yet, I'll share that if anything prepared me for the pandemic, it was going through a legal and emotional tsunami the year before that consumed all waking and sleeping moments of my life.

Actually, to be fair, if there was any blessing from the divorce, it was that my ex-husband and I both made it as fast and amicable as possible. I've likened my legal process to clipping into a spin bike; I did what I could to keep pedaling at the speed and rate of the attorneys and the court system. I know this isn't often the case.

The emotional process, though, was very different

and pretty intense. My grieving process also wasn't private, which is what I would've preferred. I live in a small town, so inevitably I'd run into a friend or acquaintance at the grocery store who'd ask the well-meaning "How are you . . . really?" I appreciated their concern, but it just seemed like I couldn't get a break from the hardship I was experiencing.

The only respite I found was in counseling, which was my sacred space for learning a whole new rubric around who I was now that I was divorced, and what I wanted my life to be now that I was the only one calling all the shots.

That latter piece really threw me for a loop, too. For nearly twenty years, I'd had a partner, a collaborator, someone to vision with and shape a future. Now it was just me, and I was the only one who was going to be contributing to my financial future, which made me feel pretty vulnerable.

Throughout my Lead Star experience, I'd always counted on my ex's salary-turned-military pension to keep our family secure. To me, it was the piece of my puzzle that I depended on to place my bets on myself to start the business. It gave me confidence that, if I failed, we wouldn't go under. Now, in this new era of life, my financial security, as well as that of my sons, was all on me. If I failed, we'd all be in trouble. The divorce had left me with less than half of my savings and the need to buy my former husband out of the house we'd built during our married life, the one my boys and I loved and wanted to keep as our home.

I remember many, many late nights, private conversations between me and myself in which I questioned my entrepreneurial pursuits as I sorted through the financial pressure. I wondered if now was the time for me to find a steady paycheck from a large employer, complete with benefits because I no longer had health insurance, so I could lead a more even, secure, predictable life. For days, I played that thought out and imagined trying on different hats— one with this employer, one with this other, one with this nonprofit—just to see how it'd feel. Yet, despite what hat I attempted, nothing seemed to fit. I wanted to wear the one I'd been wearing, the Lead Star hat I was comfortable with, the one that I loved more than anything.

I remember going out for a long walk in the woods, which is always a great communion. It dawned on me that, aside from the first few years of owning Lead Star, the business had been quite stable. Most years were growth years, so why did pursuing my current career path feel more intimidating? I didn't need the income from my ex for security (though it certainly helped and was valued). And, while I'd lost half my financial assets, I still had 100 percent of my talents. Why would I need to change jobs if the one I had was a vehicle for leveraging my talents for even greater success?

This realization clarified for me that I didn't need to make a change professionally. If anything, I needed to rely on the talents that I'd been developing in this career field and double down on those. Those exact talents were the ones that were going to help me rebuild to a place stronger than ever before. Those were the ones I needed to place my bets on. Throughout the divorce process, I'd spent too much time focused on what I was losing, both in a partnership and in dollars. Sadly, the partnership was gone and wasn't ever coming back. But the money I was losing to settle our assets was fully renewable; I'd retained all the talent and capacity to earn. That was my true safety net.

TALENT IS YOUR SAFETY NET

In our role as coaches, we see professionals who put more trust in an employer, an organization, the government, or somebody else's risk tolerance than their own talents and skills. They believe that their time in a role is what keeps them secure, or their relationship with someone in management, and if they keep their head down and do what they're told, then they will have all the security they need.

It's easy to believe that a job is part of your safety net. In reality, though, it's your performance and ability to meet and exceed standards that keeps you employed. It's not the position, it's how you grow, contribute, and perform in the role. Your talent, effort, and ability to rise strong after inevitable setbacks are key elements of your safety net. Your talent is what creates opportunity for you.

We see many professionals who go to work, do the work—good work, for that matter—but don't grow in skill and relevance. Angie's dad, Jerry, served as a career educator. During his time as a high school principal, he often noted two types of teachers:

- Those with twenty years of experience
- Those with one year of experience, repeated twenty times

We can all appreciate the nuance found in these differences, as well as our preference for how we'd want someone to characterize our workplace performance.

The challenge, of course, is what it takes to be good in today's ever-evolving professional landscape, especially with the rapid evolution of technology and changing norms around how work gets done. We, personally, must take ownership of this to stay on pace. That way, when we advocate for risks at work, we're doing so in the context of what's relevant, what's forward leaning, and what will add real value.

Many people believe that career development is an employer's responsibility. This isn't our belief. Career development is your responsibility; you can't wait for an employer to introduce you to emerging technology, new ways of collaborating and connecting, or business best practices. If they do, great! Bonus! You've got to be the one owning your development, because it's that critical to your marketability—don't delegate that responsibility to anyone. The same mentality applies to entrepreneurs, consultants, business owners, and others who don't have traditional employment. Being credible is your currency.

Future-proof your ability to contribute by staying aware of what's to come, what's currently valued, and what is growing in value. This can often be beyond just expanding skills or new technology; it could be new mindsets or priorities; it could be what competitors are doing and your company isn't. Credible leaders make sure they're not just talented now, but that their talents also have relevance for the future.

This is especially critical in today's environment because we never really know how vulnerable we are to disruption, so we need our talents to be ready when we call on them.

JUDGMENT—BUILDING YOUR ABILITY TO TRUST IN YOURSELF

The final aspect of your safety net is your judgment, which we define as your ability to weigh facts, or possible courses of action, to make sound decisions. Developing sound judgment was a key component of our training as Marines simply because so many of our choices would have significant consequences for ourselves and others. The Corps knew we were going to face much uncertainty in the missions ahead of us, and while they couldn't provide us with an answer key for the scenarios we'd encounter, they could help us improve our ability to discern what was important about what we were experiencing and how to use that information to make better choices to resolve a problem, move through a transition, or determine how best to influence an outcome.

This was incredibly valuable as the Marines knew one thing about us—we were young. We had relatively few experiences in life. People with sound judgment are either very experienced or have learned from others' experiences (or, of course, both). The Corps accelerated our education in both arenas, which is why the culture was so focused on storytelling, reading, and after-action reflection. They wanted our judgment to be as expedited as possible, so took every chance to ensure we were learning.

In the same spirit, no matter where we are in life, our experiences have been limited to what we've been exposed to; we've learned through life that one of the best things we can all do is develop continuously our secondhand experiences. By understanding the hows and whys of someone else's thinking, choices, success, or missteps, you open your mind to learning from others and gain a unique ability to recognize new truths, opportunities, and perspectives that can lead to better decisions when you place bets on you.

RISKING IN LIFE: COURTNEY'S STORY

Fresh Perspectives from Secondhand Experiences

My early forties were met with a lot of reflection. I knew I was no longer young, but as Angie would remind me, I wasn't ancient yet either.

Two distinct conversations I had during this season left a strong impression on me and have shaped both my perspective and judgment since. One took place in an office on the top floor of a stately skyscraper, and the other unfolded while I was sitting on the beach.

Let's go to the office first. I had spent the day working with the CEO of a Fortune 500 company who was in his early sixties. Connecting with him was always a great secondhand learning experience, because he was candid and specific about detailing his intent and thinking around the many choices he needed to make to lead the company into the future.

We were discussing the leadership styles of his colleagues, and he was talking specifically about a woman in his organization whom he believed needed to transition. He admired her talent, praised her contribution, and then remarked on how it would be best for her to leave the company. Sensing my surprise after hearing his glowing appraisal, he explained that she had so much talent, and "so much runway in front of her" (the woman was my age), and that she needed to be where she could level up and find new challenges. He admitted that they didn't see eye to eye on issues, yet his respect for her was strong. He wanted her to find a place where she could flourish.

I knew the woman by reputation; everything he said about her was true. I never viewed her tenure in the way he had, yet his thought process presented me with a great mental image on how to view future opportunity—a runway. I learned two weeks later that the woman the CEO was referring to had left the company. If it weren't for my conversation with him, I wouldn't have been so excited for her as I envisioned her launching into a role where she could utilize the full breadth of her talents.

Now, to the beach talk, which happened just a few weeks later. That memorable conversation was with my dad, who was in his late seventies at the time. While the sun was setting, and we were watching my younger siblings play with my kids on the beach, I was lamenting (again) that I was old, and my dad was telling me how young I was. Together we were recalling where my dad was in his early forties. After doing some quick math, we determined he was forty-two in 1980. His whole life as I know it today was just beginning. Three months after turning forty-two, he married my most amazing stepmother. At forty-two, he also only had two of his five children. He was only eleven years into the career he would retire from decades later. My dad was basically my age, and the runway ahead of him was vast.

These two conversations were enlightening for me. Not only did they offer me a refreshed perspective, but they gave me a broader view of how my choices today can launch me into new eras of growth, development, and opportunity and how much time, in fact, I'd have to experience the rewards of my choices.

While we never know exactly how many days are ahead of us, it can be quite valuable as leaders to imagine the expanse of our runways. Whether we have five years or twenty-five years until retirement, knowing that we have time to reinvent, recommit, or redo a decision is comforting. We're not stuck in time. We have the power to exercise our judgment and redirect our lives in either small or significant ways. We are only anchored in time if we choose to be.

By continuing to develop your perspective on where you are in life, your ability to bet on you by imagining what's next, what's left, or what's still in your heart to become grows. When you see the world through the vantage points and experiences of others, your ability to discern what's best for you expands as you understand and apply lessons learned. Embracing the now can also include understanding longevity, and respecting that we're all still works in progress. Success and security can be just as fleeting as fit—yet as quickly as they can vanish, they can be recreated with your talent and judgment as you make better and better bets on yourself.

STRENGTHEN YOUR JUDGMENT

To keep progressing as a leader, building the perspective and wisdom that will allow you to make the best choices for you, we encourage you to keep developing your judgment through:

- Continuously building on your knowledge base; wise choices come from the wisdom acquired through curiosity and learning.
- Being open to first- and secondhand experiences; being intentional about asking people about their roles, responsibilities, and greatest lessons learned. People want to help. Sometimes all it takes is for you to ask.
- Reflecting on your experiences, mining them for life lessons.
- Seeking outside perspectives to help inform your own; if you feel like you've got a tough choice, seek out your guides—they're there to help. No tough decision should ever be made in a vacuum.
- Connecting with your values on an ongoing basis; judgment absent your values leads to bad (and sometimes unethical) things. When your values are present in your life, they serve as self-fulfilling prophecies.

In other words, we should be in perpetual learning mode. This is really important because you never know when your judgment will be called on in your *Bet on You* journey and, when it is, you'll want it to be as primed as it can possibly be. Anticipation of challenges AND preparation for them combine very well to strengthen this element of your safety net.

Over time, our judgment allows us to form better, and often more creative, decisions when the situation demands that we heighten our effort, change, pivot, sustain, stop, or start anything new. You know, those moments when you look at yourself and say, *"What do I need to do here?"*

What's crucial, too, is that we generate not just one course of action (COA) in those moments; but we have the ability to generate multiple COAs to push our thinking and creativity in the situation. We know for many of us, we can get so fixed in our thinking when we're feeling stressed, challenged, or pressed.

These are the moments when we tend to think we can do A or B, that's it. We lose sight easily that there are many other letters in the alphabet that can represent different solutions to our problems, and, with time and consideration, we can unearth a few of those to determine what is possible and what is probable.

By *possible*, we mean what can be achieved. And by *probable*, the likelihood that it will actually happen. You need both to win with risk.

When you're in the midst of the fog of challenge, assessing the possibility and probability will help discern what's the best choice for you with what you're faced with. And when you face challenge points with just enough financial security, a strong belief in your ever-growing talent, and the knowledge that your judgment is sound (even if you'll never be able to predict the future perfectly), you'll be ready for what's ahead. That includes times when we need to rebound from setbacks, disappointments, missteps, and mistakes all leaders experience.

PUTTING IT INTO PRACTICE

- Note what you'll do to weave a strong safety net as you continue designing your personal Risk Manifesto at www.leadstar.us/bet-on-you.
- Identify the strengths and areas that need attention in your safety net (finances, talent, and judgment) so you can be more risk-ready.
- Money is a common barrier to exploring risk. Clarify what you need to feel secure financially—don't underrepresent or overexaggerate this number.
- Realize that your talent (not an entity) is what allows you to be professionally secure. Keep developing yourself and staying relevant with the times.
- Your judgment can build over time only if you're open

to learning—stay in curiosity mode, seek to learn from the experiences of others, especially the hows and whys behind the experiences they encounter.

- Leverage your judgment by pushing your thinking to discover the COA (courses of action) you can take to make your goals and dreams probable. Don't bet on *just* possible.

CHAPTER SEVEN

REALIZE WHEN YOU'RE WINNING

"We're so busy watching out for what's just ahead of us that we don't take time to enjoy where we are."

—BILL WATTERSON[1]

QUICK LOOK

An insatiable pursuit of "more" can prevent you from valuing the significance of your journey. This chapter will help you focus on how to claim the "W" in your life by fully realizing the victories you're earning.

THOUGHT STARTERS

Winning isn't about a trinket or a trophy. It's an emotion that can be cultivated internally by you with the right focus and intention.

Don't look externally for others to tell you how your success should feel.

You get to determine your path and how you experience success.

There's delight in the simple. A well-designed life has winning built into the smallest moments.

Remember when motivational posters were a thing in the corporate world? You know, the images of a team rowing in perfect sync, a drop of water making a ripple, a stoic eagle staring into the horizon. The pictures would all be set against a black backdrop and in white, uppercase letters there'd be keywords like *EXCELLENCE, TEAMWORK,* or *COMMITMENT.* Of course, these would later be the inspiration for many amusing internet memes. But back in the day? They were a pretty big deal.

These posters served as reminders that there's an opportunity every day for us to strive toward pinnacle achievements so we can feel victorious, like we're winning. And the concept of winning, too, in these images was represented in epic moments—a medal at the end of a race, a mountain summit.

These posters were—and still are—reflections of our society.

We exist in an achievement-oriented world; one in which winning is framed as fleeting and only attainable in us-versus-the-world moments when we're either defying the odds or conquering something or someone else.

The problem with the societal definition of winning is that it's overly focused on glory—not happiness, joy, contentment, and other winning qualities that are life enhancing, as well as both possible and achievable each and every day.

Our concern is that if you buy into the wrong definition of winning on your *Bet on You* journey, you'll walk right past everyday wins without experiencing the success you've already earned, as well as the pride associated with who you are, all you have, and where you're going. You need this broader type of winning; it fuels your confidence and allows you to experience fulfillment— an ever elusive quality we're seeking on our risk-taking journey that sometimes can seem so hard to find.

We're going to focus this entire chapter on how you can realize winning in your own, very personal, and very meaningful way, starting with helping you see winning from a new vantage point.

WINNING: IN ITS TRUE LIGHT

Here's a question for you: When was the last time you felt you were winning?

If you're like a lot of people, that's hard to answer. It might require you to travel back in time and think of a hard-earned accomplishment that was either accompanied by a paper certificate or some hardware, like a medal or a plaque. It's probably fair to say, too, that your win was defined by someone else as an acknowledgment for your performance, versus an internal feeling that signified something meaningful.

On the flip side: When was the last time you felt like you weren't winning? We imagine this question is easier to answer and might include times like these when:

- A relationship was in a state of neglect.
- You deferred gratification for far too long.
- You weren't feeling valued at work.
- You let down someone in your life.
- You were coming apart at the seams.
- You didn't meet a high standard you set for yourself.
- You felt numb due to burnout.

If, as you read this list, you're nodding at each bullet and checking it off mentally, thinking, *"Yep, that's me. I've been there before,"* chances are you might feel you're playing a losing game in life. We'd like to argue that's just not true. Instead, we believe the list above highlights the cost of a never-ending quest for more, rather than approaching winning in a different, less complicated way. After all, if the cost of the pursuit of success included any of the aforementioned bullets, we wonder why would anyone want to keep paying that price?

We want you to understand that winning is an emotion that captures your pride in an accomplishment, whether that accomplishment is large or small. Winning can be found so much more readily than in the narrower ways we often buy into. This isn't us declaring that everyone should get a trophy for everything they do in life; it's just that life presents us simple victories in ways that can bring us lasting joy and satisfaction.

Imagining winning as a range of opportunities gives you freedom to think of many situations in life where claiming a victory is possible. In this new light, winning might look like:

- Coordinating your busy schedule with your partner's so you two can find the time midweek to meet up for lunch.
- Escaping the city to go for a family bike ride in the country.
- Helping a client find a new use for your product or a new solution to a challenge.
- Attending financial planning classes and discovering new ways to achieve your goals.
- Organizing a community service project at work to allow you and your team to make a difference for others.
- Learning how to bake bread or cook a new dish that delights your family.

What you'll notice in this list, too, is how personal these answers are. What looks and feels like winning to one person is completely different to another. That's really important. Winning should never be defined by others; it has to be defined by you. That way you can be intentional about experiencing it and—when you do—you get to accept the host of positive emotions that come with it.

Developing your own definition of winning also helps ensure

that you're not looking externally for cues and clues on how you're doing in life. We all know people like this; those who measure success against others in pretty artificial ways. They look outside of themselves to see who's doing what, what prized items others possess. These types of benchmarks aren't healthy or helpful. They can lead to great insecurity and push us into situations where we get stuck on a treadmill that is the insatiable quest for more—more money, more achievements, more stuff to distract us from life—thinking that it's the "more" that we acquire that will make us happy.

We've met and heard of many miserable, "successful" people who've got all the stuff, but haven't understood winning broadly enough to realize that they, by themselves and in this moment, don't need "more"—they need to realize that they're enough.

RISKING IN CAREER AND LIFE: JOHN OATES

When Less Is More

When we think of musical legends Daryl Hall and John Oates, two thoughts pop into our minds:

Their music is awesome and timeless.

Whatever they've done to stay on top, it's working.

Regarding that latter point—from afar, it certainly seems this way. The duo has had thirty-four chart hits, six of which were number one hits on Billboard's Top 100. They're Rock & Roll Hall of Fame inductees. And, to top it off, they've been touring together for fifty-plus years. Any of these achievements alone is impressive. But all of them together? It's astounding.

Yet when you hear John Oates talk about his rise to fame, it doesn't sound like a victory march, despite the fact he had all the stuff that money could buy—houses, sports cars, a Learjet—and a glamorous lifestyle—model wife, late nights at Studio 54. He shares that, with every step he made toward achieving professional success, he noticed a decline in his personal life, which led him to a point where his relationships suffered. He'd lost sight of who he was and what really mattered.

His day of reckoning came when his accountants told him, bluntly, that after cutting records, recording hits, and touring for nearly two decades, he was broke—flat-out broke. This was John's tipping point to change his life.[2]

He started by selling all his possessions, except a condo in Aspen, Colorado. He pulled himself away from the music scene, an act he's described as soul cleansing.[3] He shaved his mustache, completely changing his iconic look, and took up the life of a mountain man—bike riding, skiing, hiking. He went on to remarry and start a family, and then to recording the type of music that was of significance to him.

This dramatic life change was a bet on himself; a decision that forced him out of the spotlight and into the unknown to rediscover what he valued, what was important, and what was sustainable. Eventually, he went back to touring with Daryl Hall. He also recorded solo tracks and collaborated with country and blues musicians—music not connected to his commercial success, but music that had long been part of his passion. Upon reflection, John went on to say: "You've got to pay me to leave my house, spend the night in hotels, and fly in airplanes. That's what I get paid for. Playing I actually do for free."[4]

John Oates isn't the first artist (or professional for that matter) to build an incredible body of work and achieve at the highest levels, only to discover that along the way they lost sight of the little things in life that create happiness and fulfillment.

The good news in this for all of us is that often what's required to get back to "good" isn't a fast trip to rock bottom so we can start over; it's the realization that a better, broader kind of winning is needed, and small, subtle changes can bring it back into our lives.

WE NEED OUR WINS

In chapter three, you dreamed of some great goals for yourself. These matter. Your pursuit of hope and greater success is important, it's inspiring. We want you to pay attention to the word *pursuit*. On your risk-taking journey, it's never the achievement that fulfills you. It's the journey. The small ways we can recognize how we're already winning in life enriches our daily life. It also has the potential to change our life, too.

Cognitive neuroscientist Ian Robertson has researched the effects of winning and explains that success shapes us more powerfully than genetics and drugs. In fact, his research has shown that when we feel like we're winning, we get a great boost in our brains from the chemicals testosterone and dopamine that help us create new ways of thinking and imagining our worlds. He claims that success is the greatest brain changer that humanity has ever known. And when you change your brain, everything changes. Remember that thoughts become beliefs, which become behaviors? Winning has the power to help you change your thoughts and see yourself as the hero of your life story, not the victim, not the innocent bystander. The actual hero, something we all want to be.

Being a hero isn't about being a braggart. As in a good fiction story, being a hero means being a protagonist—you're the one driving the story toward a better outcome and getting the encouragement by your small wins along the way. Our hope for you is that you start thinking of winning as an enduring concept, versus a chase toward fleeting moments.

RISKING IN CAREER: ANGIE'S STORY

Success Shouldn't Feel Like a Chore

When Courtney and I set out to start our company, we had big dreams. Some were quantifiable—revenue targets, clients acquired, book sales. Others were more about the experience of it all. We had this fantasy of a jet-setting life, one where we'd be rushing through airports, cabbing to five-star hotels, wearing designer clothes, eating amazing meals at famous restaurants, and facilitating meetings in elaborate office spaces.

Within a few years, the success we'd dreamed of was becoming a reality. Our clients were flying us all over the world to consult with their organizations and support them in developing leaders at all levels. The audiences for our keynote addresses were getting larger, and our first book, *Leading from the Front,* was continuing to produce strong sales. We were on our way for sure. The challenge, though, was the pace. We were moving fast and spent more time living in the future, imagining what needed to be next, versus savoring all that was happening in the now. That prevented us from reaping the joy of the present by realizing our wins, like the simple stuff that we worked so hard for and wanted in our life—quiet time at home, watching our kids play sports without the distraction of technology, or even getting our holiday cards out on time.

Soon, our ambitions started to feel less like an adventure and more like a chore. (Business clothes require dry cleaning; after trips, it was just one more thing we had to do. I call this "Life Admin"—I hate Life Admin and the errands and to-dos that come with it.) While it looked like we were climbing up the ladder of success, what was really happening was we were on a treadmill . . . at an incline. Not the upward mobility we were hoping for.

The good news is that Courtney and I realized something was off pretty quickly. That's the benefit of a friendship within a business partnership; our conversations weave between life and work, and we're quick to notice similar trends and patterns—like, "It looks like we should be winning, but this feels awful and we're not having any fun anymore. We need to change."

Together we confronted the challenge, pushing us to think how we wanted our success to feel. Not what we wanted it to be, like as a goal. But more abstractly.

This realization led us to focus on bringing back simple joys to our work. I say *bringing*, but it was really *forcing*. It's hard to break habits, especially ones that require you to slow down. On our work trips, we'd build in time to visit a local museum, walk at a park near our hotel, or even just order take-out and spend some time alone in our hotel room—something to bring quiet to days that were full of connecting with new people. We started building stronger boundaries between our work and home lives, as well as respecting the boundaries each other built. We brainstormed about how we could unplug more fully the day after returning from a whirlwind trip. We started saying "no" to back-to-back projects that left us barely enough time to do our laundry and repack our suitcases.

We've learned that dreams and goals are valuable; they set you on an exciting course. But equally as important is imagining how you want your success to feel when you get there—burned out or invigorated? We all want the latter. Dreams and goals will change—winning, and its spirit, doesn't have to. To keep the feeling of a win in your life, the idea is simple—be as intentional with your emotions as you are with your life direction.

IMAGINE HOW YOU WANT SUCCESS TO FEEL

We need to recognize winning for what it is—an inside game. And a good place to start doing this is reflecting on what winning is to you—the large and small of it—and then thinking about how you'd like your success to feel. As Angie just shared, this feeling changes over time.

As you take risks, we want them to lead you to somewhere good that feels good along the way.

It takes a little bit of experience to know how you want success to feel for you. Knowing what you don't like leads you to discovering what you do. It also takes reflection and awareness, as you think about where you are right now.

We'd like you to take a look at the two columns below. As you read each pair of words, consider what column you spend more time in *right now:*

Gratitude	Jealousy
Love	Indifference
Serenity	Chaos
Awe	Numb
Hope	Resignation
Pride	Insecurity
Curiosity	Righteousness
Satisfaction	Discontent
Amusement	Bitterness
Inspiration	Beat-down
Acceptance	Resentment
Empathy	Judgment

The left-hand column is obviously the goal—these qualities, when experienced, are where joy and fulfillment can be found. That's what winning looks like! Yet, let's be real. It takes energy, focus, and commitment to get there. We're not hardwired for gratitude; resentment is easier to feel than acceptance, and some of us are so busy that we identify more with numbness than we do awe.

If you're discovering that you're spending a lot of time on the right-hand side of the house, maybe it's time to audit your days. If you can't remember the last two weeks because they were a busy blur of work, logistics, challenge, and exhaustion, caution: you're not going to feel like you're winning. (As if you didn't know that, right?)

If your last two weeks don't meet your definition of success, think more about what to leave out rather than what to add in, to allow you the space to realize you're winning. Less is always better. Savoring simple joys isn't possible when you're operating at a breakneck pace. Finding a sustainable pace makes realizing you're winning more possible.

The left-hand qualities take a lot of work, emotionally, to get to. And, when you get there, it takes even more work to stay there. It's part of the disciplines of winning that are important to embrace, which include:

- Sleeping well. It's easier to be happy when we're well rested.
- Noticing nature. There's so much to wonder at outside. Take the time to pick your head up, find a window, and spend a moment just seeing what's outside. If you can, go for a walk. These meditative practices create tiny moments of rejuvenation.
- Staying fully present. How often are your mind and body in totally different places? Work to eliminate distractions (like your phone) from moments when you need to be present.
- Eating mindfully. Eating on the run often puts us in a position to be numb to our wins. Plus, our food choices diminish when it's grab and go. If you don't have time to

savor a meal, your likelihood of having time to feel the positive emotions with nourishment decreases.

- Banishing guilt. Guilt is kryptonite to joy. The moment you feel it, hold the space for understanding why and work through those reasons to a place beyond it. Excessive guilt burdens your opportunities to win. Examine this warning sign and work on those changes, which can often mean letting go of unrealistic standards for yourself.
- Connecting deeply. Seek to spend as much time engaging with people as you spend task focused. Ordinary days can become extraordinary days if you allow connections to flourish.
- Don't "busy" your life unnecessarily. If you have a free evening, or an unplanned Saturday, don't schedule something just to keep busy. Be okay with being still. Winning is often found in these moments.

If you discover that these tactics are adding value but still aren't doing the trick, here's an option for you: Consider a risk-rest.

RISK-REST: THE BREAK
YOU SOMETIMES NEED

Breaking news: You're not a machine. Just like athletes plan for an off-season that strengthens them for peak performance, don't let your off-seasons sneak up on you. Be intentional about planning for surge periods by appreciating the intensity they bring, knowing they need to be followed by rest. If, for example, you went to night school for three years to finish your degree, and all the while you took care of your family and excelled as a student, after graduation plan time and space with less responsibility or achievement as you prepare for the next season. Pause the pursuit to recover, relax, and be rejuvenated by stillness instead of motion. Pacing well is an important part of sustainable, enjoyable winning.

On the same note, whenever a friend or colleague alerts us that he or she has accepted a new role with a different company, our first question is, "How long are you going to take off between jobs?" If they say anything less than two weeks, they'll get a stern note of caution from us reminding them that space and rest are key components of kickstarting their new role with renewed vigor. Less than two weeks often just isn't enough. Besides, we reason, when in life do you get a monthlong break? If you can take it, take it.

Throughout this book, we're talking about goals, dreams, hopes, and stepping into uncertainty. Nothing about our message says you've got to be a goal-junkie who fails to appreciate life. We need our rest so we can be our best. Think of it this way: If you don't take a vacation and lose vacation days each year, you're doing a tremendous disservice to yourself, your team, your family, and your employer. Trust us—it's better for everyone, especially yourself, when you take the time to renew.

While you might take one big vacation a year, give yourself permission to take some smaller periods off—a day trip here or a holiday celebration there. Spread your time off. Don't just plan for those marathon moments throughout a lifetime or else you risk burnout, frustration, and misery. Besides, you should never run a marathon right before you run a marathon. A constant pursuit is overrated and stunts your ability to find joy in the simple wonders of your days. Lasting success requires intentional risk-rests.

DISCOVERING JOY IN THE SIMPLE

A successful *Bet on You* journey often takes patience, persistence, and a commitment to discovering a steady rhythm that'll allow you to bring risk-taking into your daily life and find joy in the smallest of experiences.

Steadiness doesn't seem exciting, does it? Even the word *simple* can sound boring. It doesn't have to be.

A life well-lived isn't really about how many mountaintops you summit, it's more about how fully you embraced climbs, experienced life at the base camps, and how well you managed the descents and plateaus. Sure, summits are exciting; but they're brief, temporary, and special states—not everyday states. Deeper satisfaction comes with being just as mindful of the terrain on the mountain you're on. Being able to delight in the rhythm of day-to-day life is a much more valuable skill than knowing how to celebrate magnificent achievement.

EXPERIENCE YOUR SUCCESS

When you do reach a mountaintop moment, though, make sure you pick your head up and be present enough to enjoy the view. This is a personal process, and it fuels confidence. Take time to reflect what got you there; understand the factors that led you to that success and which ones can and should be repeated. Lessons learned can be mined, too, from the obstacles you encountered that you want to avoid in the future:

- What did I do (or stop doing) to create this win?
- What talents or strengths made winning possible?
- How can I use what I learned for future success?
- What did I overcome to achieve the win? (Naming what

you overcame is an important reminder of the capability and capacity you've gained for the future.)

• What lessons did I learn that I can apply going forward?

Remember, realizing when you're winning means you're not seeking perfection achieved, you're seeking to recognize progress, momentum, accomplished in the context of predominant joy and satisfaction.

RISKING FOR IMPACT: COURTNEY'S STORY

A New Perspective Changes the View

So much of the early days of Lead Star can be summed up in the classic line from Jimmy Buffett's song, "Changes in Attitudes, Changes in Latitudes": "Reading departure signs in some big airport reminds me of the places I've been." As Angie shared, life was in constant motion as we built Lead Star, so much so that I was often unaware of when we were surging forward or realizing a win.

One airport memory crystalizes this lack of awareness. It took place during a time when one of our biggest clients was just a mere start-up itself. This tech company was focused on making the world more open and connected. To do so, they knew that their teams needed to have leaders at all levels and be aware of what it took to achieve shared victories as they were forging new ground, creating a platform that was quickly being embraced by the masses. The company was Facebook. Not Facebook as you know it today, but Facebook as a scrappy band of a little more than 150 employees and very little limelight.

As was typical in those days, I found myself slumped in a metal-lined, black leather airport waiting area seat at LaGuardia Airport. With the armrest bar digging into my back as I impossibly tried to prop myself up in a comfortable way, sitting sideways in the seat, feet flung over the other armrest. I was on the phone with my favorite Uncle Jack, a great mentor and supporter of mine. I was detailing my time in New York City. Angie and I'd spent several days working with Facebook's New York team, including a couple of leaders who'd been very successful at Google, prior to their time with the new venture.

The wealth we'd just witnessed was staggering. One of our workshops for junior managers had been hosted in the home of a senior executive. Her home was a gorgeous, two-story penthouse apartment in SoHo, complete with its own elevator entrance and multiple balconies with beautiful city views. And, while the apartment was magnificent, that wasn't the detail I was recounting to my uncle. Instead, I was sharing how much I respected the humility and sense of service these particular executives had brought to the experience. They were so open to learning, so willing to engage, and so focused on getting the small details in their home right for their junior team members, most of whom were quite young, broke, and exhausted from long hours of doing whatever they could to progress the company forward.

I was laughing with my uncle, sharing how I thought the more senior managers would've been anything but the concerned, conscientious, compassionate people I had the pleasure of working with that day.

After lecturing me just a bit on stereotyping (thanks, Uncle Jack!), our conversation shifted to a more serious tone as I shared a bit about the insecurity I was feeling. It came across mostly through questions I was really asking myself but were posed to my uncle. "Will great success ever really happen for me? Do I have what it takes?" I went on to express, "Those people have achieved so much already, and they are really trying to change the world for the better. I wonder if I'll ever be able to contribute in that way." The line fell silent for a moment as I waited for my uncle's response.

Out of the silence came a series of questions in response. "Well, Courtney, who was it that the Facebook team hired to advise them on leadership development? They could hire anyone. Which company are they trusting with developing their employees?" That caught my attention. My uncle continued, "I don't think you see it. You already are successful. You are advising great people who are doing bold things. You're a great person, doing bold things. I can't tell you if you'll ever be lottery-winning rich, but don't doubt that you are making a difference. You're having impact."

That conversation is so easy to recall today, because it was a true "aha" moment for me. In many ways, my life up until that point had been a chase. A fun, invigorating, high-speed, high-adrenaline adventure (especially my time as a Marine) for sure, but a chase nonetheless. I was always in motion, on my way to a destination, not even considering that I might have arrived already. In this case, I was clearly on a mountaintop, but I couldn't see it. Sometimes we need others in our life giving us a good solid nudge to pick our heads up and realize where we are.

While I didn't know it fully at the time, I'm sure about it today: I bet on myself so I can support, coach, and develop others to do the same. That's my purpose, that's my mission. In understanding that, I can now see more clearly when I'm winning. Just as I can see better where I've stumbled, fallen off course, and experienced setbacks—typically times when I was focused on the pursuit of some new prize versus on the journey to contribute.

Today I still absolutely enjoy climbing. I have goals, ambitions, hopes, and dreams. We all do. Yet I am no longer chasing something. Instead, I embrace the fleeting view on the mountaintop, savoring and recognizing those special moments. And I value the descent since I know it brings me to another plateau of preparation—by choice, not randomly. That's winning. Know what matters most to you and allow the cycle of seasons to bring you closer to joy, satisfaction, and contribution—not further away from those success-sustaining factors.

LASTING, JOYFUL SUCCESS

Ultimately your *Bet on You* journey isn't about creating one-hit-wonder moments—it's about imagining and creating richer experiences. The purpose of life is to live it. That means recognizing and embracing the smallest and quietest of wins along the way. By being intentional about how you'd like to win, how you want those victories to feel, and by noticing all the small, simple joys along the way, you'll find yourself enjoying great mountain-top moments and the seasons of rest and preparation that create them.

PUTTING IT INTO PRACTICE

- Take time to note what small wins look like for you through your Risk Manifesto at www.leadstar.us /bet-on-you.

- Remember that winning is an emotion. It's found in the large and small achievements that make you proud of yourself.
- Define winning for yourself. Don't look externally, as that will lead to an insatiable quest for more.
- Experience your success by noting your wins and celebrating them internally. This practice builds your confidence and fuels your happiness.
- Wins can be loud or they can be quiet. Don't neglect or overlook the quiet ones; they allow you to realize all that you have each and every day.
- Understand what winning feels like; know, too, that the success you aspire to today can look/feel different when you achieve it.
- When grand things happen (like mountaintop moments), be sure to pick your head up and savor the view.

CHAPTER EIGHT

PLAN FOR THE FEARS AND FAILS

"Most great people have attained their greatest success just one step beyond their greatest failure."

—NAPOLEON HILL

QUICK LOOK

This chapter focuses on what you need to do when you encounter fear and failure—they're not the same thing, but they swing in the same circles. Having a strategy will allow you to know what to do when you meet them.

THOUGHT STARTERS

Your fears are real and healthy, though they can be disproportionate to the threats you perceive. Know your fears, but don't let them own you.

We tend to think of fails as catastrophic; yet fails come in all shapes and sizes. When you fail, the best way to respond is to learn, adapt, and apply.

Resiliency is the gift you gain from moving past your fears and learning from your failures. Embrace the upsets and value the imperfections life gives you—not only do they make you unique, how you handle them determines your success.

W e want you to visualize your success. Imagine it so clearly that you take note of where you're at, what you're doing in the moment, and even what you're wearing. Don't just visualize it once, either. Visualize it often, because the more you think about the reality of your achievement, the more likely it is to translate into a possibility.

Visualization is a powerful technique practiced by the most extraordinary of athletes, business moguls, thought leaders, and influencers around the world. Katie Ledecky,[1] a seven-time Olympic gold-medal winner and world record–breaking swimming champ, has claimed to visualize her success down to how each stroke should feel during her races. Jim Carrey,[2] another famed visualization practitioner, not only imagines his success repeatedly, but before his big break he wrote himself a check for $10 million for "acting services rendered" and carried it around in his wallet until it actually happened. (He later cleared that amount for his role in *Dumb and Dumber.*)

Our imaginations hold so much power over what we experience. And while it's important to visualize the success you want on your *Bet on You* journey, it's also just as critical that you think about your fears and what fails you might encounter. Not to dwell on them, but to acknowledge and plan how you'll handle them when they appear.

Tennis legend Billie Jean King[3] has often shared that before matches she'd spend time thinking about all the things that could go wrong and how she'd respond, as well as all the things that could happen that were beyond her control. She also focused specifically on her side of the net—not her opponent's—knowing that if success was possible, it'd be within her control. And when mistakes happened, as they inevitably would, she'd focus on letting them go and not allowing them to influence what happened next.

On your risk-taking journey, we want you to prepare for all the amazing things that will come into your life through the choices you make. We also want you to plan for two big F words in your life—*fear* and *failure*—because they will inevitably be a part of your journey, too. And when these two f'n dream killers appear, often hand in hand, we want you to have a plan for them, so you're not paralyzed or imprisoned by them.

THE F'N DREAM KILLERS

Fear and failure—they're not the same thing, but they certainly swing in the same circles.

Fear is a primal emotion triggered by the thought that someone or something is risky or dangerous and could likely cause us harm or pain. While our fears can be healthy, they're often not proportionate to the threats we face. As an example:

Your odds of being attacked by a shark are 1 in 3.75 million.[4] Your odds of dying in a car crash are 1 in 103.[5] We want to know: What are you more afraid of?

(We're more afraid of sharks, too.)

Our fears can, clearly, also be irrational, yet they're there to inform us that the possibility of failure is certain. Failure is, after all, our shared number one fear.

When we talk about failure, we often think of catastrophic loss, though there are many shades of failure. It can be felt when we're embarrassed, make mistakes or missteps, or when we experience disappointments or setbacks. For example:

- Your family makes the final rounds of an adoption process and isn't selected.
- You poured hours into a proposal, and it didn't win the bid.

- You spent a weekend working to organize your house, and you didn't make it past the garage.
- You "replied all" to an email meant for just one reader (and what you wrote should never have been expressed in an email).

The dictionary defines *failure* broadly as the "lack of success." In this case, there are probably failure moments we encounter every day. What's key, though, is how you think about fears and failures, which comes down to how you choose to experience them. This will inevitably determine your relationship with them and, more important, the outcome.

RISKING IN CAREER: ANGIE'S STORY

The Stairway to Heaven

Officer Candidate School in Quantico, Virginia, is the training ground for all aspiring Marine Corps officers. I attended my six-week OCS experience the summer between my junior and senior year in college. Preparing for OCS was no small task; I'd spent three years in the Naval Reserve Officer Training Corps at the University of Michigan studying military history, understanding the Marine Corps culture, and getting physically ready for the rigors of this sleep-depriving, long-marching, grueling program. If I didn't pass the program, one where nearly 50 percent of all women don't, I'd not only have to pay back my academic scholarship, I'd have to deal with this blowing fail for the rest of my life. The latter seemed worse.

I was the only female in my NROTC program who, at the time, wanted to be a Marine. The others were headed to the Navy. So, alongside my Marine option male midshipmen, I'd wake up three days a week at 5:00 a.m., and we'd go out for long runs, climb ropes until our arms ached, and do endless sit-ups to prepare for the physical aspects of OCS, all before our classes started.

I felt as ready as I possibly could be by the time I arrived at OCS, because I spent so much time training over my head. Being able to hang with my ROTC crew gave me the confidence and courage I needed to believe I could pass the physical challenges. But as I became oriented with the OCS training grounds and started seeing all the obstacles that we'd have to surmount in order to graduate, I started to become nervous, because many of them represented challenges that I couldn't do anything to prepare for, obstacles designed with the average man's height in mind—five feet nine inches. I'm short. Really short, five feet three inches. You can always become stronger, but you can't train for tall.

The Stairway to Heaven, in particular, was visually intimidating, but as I learned more about the challenge it became frightening. It's a ladder made of wood logs that stands thirty feet tall, straight up in the air. What's unique about the rungs is that the ones on the bottom are close together. As you work your way to the top, they're spread farther apart. Your task, as a candidate, is to climb up one side and, when you get to the top log, roll your body over it, and then climb down the other side.

On course day, we're all reminded that there'd be nothing to support us going up and going down. We were also advised to be careful, as one slip would lead to a broken back. I loved how nonchalantly our instructors offered that up, as if a broken back was on par with a splinter.

As I "admired" the obstacle at its base, it was pretty clear to me that to clear that top log, I couldn't reach up, grab it, then roll over it. I'd have to jump up and catch it, muster all the strength I had to hurl my legs over it, and finally, as my arms hung onto the top log for dear life, my feet would need to flail in midair as they searched for the log below that'd lead me to my descent.

I was afraid. Very afraid. It wasn't just physical fear, either. A broken back also meant broken dreams. I wouldn't earn my commission in the Marines, my post-college plan. I'd have to share this embarrassing experience with friends and family. The additional upsets and consequences of not overcoming the obstacle filled my mind, quickly. There were just too many to count.

But I knew one thing: Whatever I focused on in that moment was going to get my attention. Our instructors had told us repeatedly throughout training that everything is mind over matter: If you don't mind, it don't matter. If I focused on my fears and the fails that would ensue, my chances for success would be limited. If I focused on the moment and what needed to be done, I'd have the courage to brave success.

Quitting, for me, was not an option, so I did what

I had to do—faced my fears rung by rung. I made my way up the first several rungs without a problem. But the closer I got to the top, the more thoughts about danger slipped into my mind as I stretched a little farther to grab the next rung. I made the conscious choice to dismiss them as quickly as they came. *Don't think about that now, Angie. Focus on right now and what's right next.* I'd clear the next log, and then the next one, a little more strain with each log passed. When I finally stood on the second to last rung, I looked up at the top log, took a deep breath, and knew I was as ready as I'd ever be. Before I made the jump, I reminded myself what I'd come here to do. I told myself that this obstacle wasn't going to be what stopped my Marine Corps career and, with everything I had, I jumped, grabbed hold of the log, and wasted no time forcing my body over it. When my first foot found the log it needed for stability on the other side, I sighed in relief so loudly, I'm sure the instructors heard it down below.

I spent hours grappling with the fear associated with the stairway, yet conquering it took only seconds. And the pride I picked up from this moment? Well, that'll last forever. When I got to the bottom of the obstacle, I couldn't help but pause and feel amazed by what just happened. Naturally, one of our drill instructors saw my smile, and barked at me, "What are you so happy about, candidate? Keep moving. GO!" While I certainly snapped to and did what I was told, I also filed that moment in my mind, knowing I'd want to recall it many times later in life when faced with fear of any kind, because I knew what I'd need to do—dig in. The feelings of victory are more than worth the discomfort of tackling your fears. And even more important, if you don't own your fears, they can control the outcomes you experience right to the point of making failure likely.

STRATEGIES TO MOVE THROUGH FEAR AND PLAN FOR FAILURE

Our fears are, most definitely, real. So is the power of our attention in the moments when we feel them. When you're experiencing the sensations that signal you're afraid, don't let them hijack your focus and consume you. Rather, employ strategies to allow you to manage them, rationalize them, and rightsize them. This will allow you to work through them on your *Bet on You* journey, so you experience the success that awaits you on the other side of what scares you.

Strategy 1: Save Your "Perfect" for Never

The fear of imperfection can invoke procrastination at best, and stop a dream in its track at worst. We've met self-proclaimed perfectionists who:

- Were afraid to apply for a role because they needed just one more experience.
- Didn't buy their first home because they couldn't find the exact, right one.
- Never launched their Etsy business because their work still wasn't good enough.

We've talked about goal attainment throughout this book as a series of steps that involve missteps, mistakes, experiments and tries, starts and stops, and step backs to step forward. Betting on you isn't a neat, straightforward, perfect process. If you're a perfectionist, you may fear risk-taking, because doing nothing could seem like a better idea than doing something that may not turn out right—by "right," we mean by your often-too-high, and sometimes impossible-to-meet, standards.

When it comes to betting on you, abandon your perfectionist goals. They're futile and unrealistic. Instead, plan and prepare for the goals you've identified for yourself in your kaleidoscope with reality in mind. Strive for good enough. We have a saying here at Lead Star: Our good enough is pretty damn great. This forces us to take action when we feel that we're applying a perfectionist standard to something that just can't be perfected. And if we feel there's a chance that we'll learn more in our journey and further perfect the idea along the way? Then, hey, great, we'll apply an iterative development mindset. Good enough is a reliable gateway to the path to greatness.

There will be things you're afraid of on your journey. There will be areas and activities that you won't be good at. Uncertainty can be maddening. Be aware, but don't fear imperfection. If you still feel the need to try to perfect something, perfect your response to managing your perfectionist tendencies—the effort you invest in knowing how to squelch them will give you the courage to move through them.

Strategy 2: War-Game Your Fears

We're Sun Tzu devotees. If you're not familiar with *The Art of War,* it's never too late to pick up a copy and absorb the wisdom and philosophies of this ancient Chinese general whose guidance is applicable to warfighting, business, and everything in between. His work reminds us that: "If you know the enemy and know yourself, you need not fear the result of a hundred battles."

We talked about self-awareness in chapter two, the "know

yourself" aspect of this quote. But what about your fears? How well do you know those enemies?

It's near impossible to conquer the unknown. On your *Bet on You* journey, get to the brass tacks of it, make a list of what scares you, what you're nervous about, and how the emotion of uncertainty makes you feel. Know that it's common to feel everything that you've identified; we've yet to meet any warrior who doesn't fight scared.

Fear is healthy; familiarity with fears allows you to rightsize them to ensure you're not overblowing them. Your fears also are an indicator that you respect the challenge that you're up against, aren't too cocky or confident in the face of it, and that your direct action is needed to move through them.

Unchecked fears, though, aren't healthy, especially when they run rampant. What's usually behind these are complex feelings of worry, insecurity, lack of worthiness, or long-held doubts (often planted by someone else, but long accepted by you without question).

If you don't sort and confront what you're afraid of, your fears can amplify and easily rule your life since the feelings build on how often you experience them. This is called *potentiation* and can manifest in many unproductive, unhelpful ways. For example, if you're worried about losing your job, even the most uneventful meeting with your boss can trigger a fear response. Or if you're nervous about the new selling method you're using in your sales role, one lukewarm comment from a customer about your product—not your method—can send you sideways.

Once you've got your fears named, war-game them. Like Billie Jean King did, imagine how you'll handle them when you meet them, all of them. See yourself navigating them, stepping beyond them, and experiencing success despite them. The mental war games make you feel rehearsed and prepared. Businesses do this all the time in the continuity of operations planning. We need to do this in our life.

Beyond the benefit of planning how to step through your fears, war-gaming allows you to set your boundaries, the lines you won't cross on your journey, because you've had a chance to visualize what your fears and potential fails can look like. Some fails you'll be fine with absorbing. Then there will be times in your thought experiments when you'll realize other fails you just can't accept.

In the military, we call this establishing go-no-go criteria. In other words, if we can push beyond our fears and find ourselves on our journey, our go-no-go criteria is there to govern whether we should persist (go!), or relent (no go!).

When we started our business, having go-no-go criteria allowed us to test both the viability and sustainability of our business. In the early years, if we didn't meet certain revenue targets, we knew we'd need to close up shop because we wouldn't last. Later, when we were exceeding targets and working around the clock to meet client demands, we established new go-no-go criteria to meet is-it-worth-it? goals, which were more related to the idea that if we lost our life to our business, then what's the point of it all?

Your go-no-go criteria helps you understand when you need to evoke courage, informs you of when you need to heighten and sustain effort, and often indicates when you need to yield because success, at least the way you envisioned, isn't going to be achieved.

And when the latter happens, success can't be achieved, you need to employ the next strategy because fails hurt. There's no way around it. And, paradoxically, fails can be the greatest gifts we receive in life because of all the learning and growth they offer that gives us an opportunity to build resiliency. The hard thing, though, when you're failing, is believing in the value of the experience so much so that you lean into it by telling yourself, *"My future self is going to be so grateful for all the suffering I'm enduring right now."*

Strategy 3: Plan for Fails

We celebrate fails when we're exercising. Broken down, torn muscles are the typical precursor to stronger, more durable ones. We can value this notion as it relates to life in the gym, but it's a concept really difficult to put into practice in the rest of our lives. In other words, push our life to failure points so we can grow.

No one likes to fail. Yet, there's so much good that can come from a bad situation. It's like the Japanese art of Kintsugi. It's the process in which broken pottery is restored by mending the pieces together with lacquer that's mixed with powdered gold, silver, or any other fine element. It's a beautiful art form born from imperfection. In fact, it's the near-perfect symbol of resilience.

We want you to prepare for fails, plan for them to happen. Not plan for specific events to fail, like "I'm going to blow this client meeting on Tuesday." That'd be defeatist. You should approach your client meeting prepared, rehearsed, and confident that you can crush it. If it doesn't work out your way, though, you need to have a plan of attack on what you'll do so that fails don't influence future successes.

A simple fail plan is to learn, adapt, and apply.

Simply stated, that is. Like anything in life, it's easier said than done.

Failure that's repeated is foolish; that means learning didn't happen. You had the experience but didn't get the benefit from the mistake. Next, learning without changing is pointless; what's the point of knowing better and not adapting? Changing without application means you miss out on the opportunity to express growth from the experience.

One fail shouldn't influence another. If you had a bad meeting, you had a bad meeting—learn, adapt, apply and make the next meeting better. There's no need to create and carry your baggage around with you. Also, don't be tempted to associate unconnected fails. One bad meeting followed by a flat tire the next day doesn't mean that the world is conspiring against you. These are two separate, unrelated situations.

Yet, in the same breath, if you're noticing repeated mistakes, missteps, and small warning signs related to a specific area of your life, like your past several meetings haven't gone as planned, then perhaps it's time to pay attention. The rare, catastrophic, unrecoverable failure usually comes with plenty of warning signs. When you see them, you have options—you can:

- Accelerate your learning, adapting, and applying.
- Pivot with or without grace.
- Do nothing and risk going down with the ship.

Notice that none of these options include placing blame. That's not leadership behavior and, besides, excuses only satisfy those who give them.

It's a delicate walk, we know, to understand when to persist and when to relent. Yet, the more attuned and accountable you are to your missteps, the better presence and judgment you can exercise in those moments when a good, solid decision is needed. Like, the decision to quit.

RISKING IN CAREER: COURTNEY'S STORY

The Power of the Quit

One of the most valuable lessons I've learned in recent years is that sometimes you have to quit something you've started, which runs contrary to how I was raised. My parents always told me to persevere, hang in, and try harder when the going gets tough.

It was great advice until I got to a certain point in my career where the complexity of the challenge I was navigating expanded significantly. The idea of quitting was tough to wrap my head around when I first considered it. After all, I invest deeply in the commitments I make. I learned, though, quitting shouldn't be an option when something's difficult. You should only quit when it sucks.

By *sucks*, I mean that either the suffering isn't worth the effort, or what you set out to achieve isn't going to happen, or if you feel that, to continue, you'll have to compromise something important—your values, your integrity. I now know that, whenever I feel this way, a graceless pivot is required.

I once had to gracelessly pivot out of a role I was excited to pivot into—serving in the C-suite for a client. The company was in a position to scale rapidly and was facing the normal challenges and friction associated with success. Through my consulting work with the company, I grew to respect the founder who was leading the way. His talent and vision were clear and inspiring. When we discussed the idea of me temporarily augmenting his team, which required moving my family to Europe, it was exciting and fear-inducing all at once. I had taken many risks professionally before, yet none that would directly involve and disrupt my family life so much. Surprisingly, my family didn't see it as a disruption. Everyone was excited at the thought of living in the United Kingdom for a short period.

I went into the endeavor hoping for the best, but having helped many companies scale, I was also acutely aware that failure was possible. When I began working inside the company, I quickly realized several inefficiencies. Revenue was growing, but recent successes had inspired a wave of hiring that led to excessive overhead costs and confusing work processes. This wasn't alarming or surprising, but it did lead to layoffs across our global offices. I also supported developing a new strategy for the business, which was an exciting, engaging process due to the many bright minds at the table. Times were challenging, but there was a lot of hope, and the will to act swiftly made success seem highly possible.

When it seemed our trajectory was back on track, a huge surprise hit. The company was rocked with scandal during the early stages of the #MeToo movement. I won't go into detail, but will share there were several allegations that we needed to take seriously. Due to my high-trust relationship with the CEO, after many hours of deep discussions, he also understood why I was advocating for an independent, legal investigation and engagement with a highly respected public relations firm. This was an added expense, and it did invite exposure, but I felt strongly that healthy companies are transparent. I felt we owed our employees that.

I knew the company had the opportunity to reckon with its past, learn from the experience, and move forward better off. Yet this would require tremendous humility and commitment to doing the right thing, as uncomfortable as it was. While I sensed our CEO was up for that journey, some of the shareholders were not. They wanted to protect the business, as well as many of the accused, and were deeply offended by the whole "hearsay" scenarios. This put them at deep odds with how I was advising the company to proceed.

I realized that leaving the company sooner than planned was becoming a possibility. This was significant for my family and Lead Star. We had a multimillion-dollar contract with the client that covered the costs of my role, and our team's engagement with strategy, leadership development, and cultural change initiatives. There was a significant financial cost to this potential quit.

Amid the swirl of everything, the CEO and I met on a Sunday to get real with one another. I shared non-negotiable concerns I had about financial practices within the company, my opinion on several conflicts of interest within the business, and steps we needed to take to ensure the legitimacy of our crisis response to the allegations. We also talked openly about my employment and the Lead Star contract in place. I left our hours-long exchange believing we'd had a full meeting of the minds. While it had not been my intent to offer ultimatums of any kind, I realized that with the clarity and specificity of our conversations, if certain actions weren't taken, I'd need to leave the company.

In the days following the conversation, commitments the CEO had made in our meeting were broken. I didn't want to resign my role, but I had no choice. I transitioned as swiftly as possible, trying not to cause too many waves in operations.

The change was abrupt, especially from the outside looking in. But I'd run out of pathways and had quickly escalated to the nuclear option, because I had to fail fast and fail forward. The aftermath of this extremely difficult choice was also exceedingly difficult. I had to minimize the impact of the decision on my family by holding in the United Kingdom long enough to allow my kids to transition well. Angie and I had to rebuild Lead Star after letting go of the lucrative contract with the company. There was no easy way out; the only way through the grief related to loss and disappointment is the practical cleanup work from the mess left behind.

Today, with the hindsight of the rest of the story, I still catch myself wishing it had turned out differently. It didn't. When I look back, it's with an eye for how I could have led better in the circumstances. By understanding what more I could've done, or how different I could have done it, there is value both for today and in the future. That doesn't change my choice; I'd do it again in the same situation, though I would've worked harder to find a way to do it differently.

Failure isn't final. It's one small chapter in your very great book of life. We must be willing to embrace the inevitable seasons of setbacks that come from the pursuit of our hopes, goals, and dreams by growing from them and continuing to step forward. I'm not a failure. I'm a leader who has failed many times. Each time, I've emerged better off for the experience and more capable of reaching toward bigger dreams.

GRIEVE THE LOSS

Leveraging fails as learning experiences means fully embracing the aftershocks and the emotions associated with something that doesn't go as planned. Let grief happen; don't fight it, don't minimize it. Clarify what's significant about your loss and feel it. You don't get the reward of the experience if you can't process the significance of the loss.

Grief isn't a linear process. It can't be multitasked or calendared like another to-do on your schedule. And there's no one "right" way to experience it, you just have to be present for it to get the benefit. This is a challenge for the time-starved, achievement-oriented individuals who like to move through life *fast*. (Remember chapter one—*slow is smooth, and smooth is fast?*) There's no life hack that allows you to cheat grief.

But there are life-helps. Like the ability to control what you can control, which helps you to focus your efforts. You can't control others, or externalities, but you can always control your response to situations.

You can also build your capability to detach and reframe. When a negative experience pops up in your mind, it's quite easy to apply negative emotions to it and replay it in your mind again and again. That's dangerous territory, though, because that's rumination, which causes excessive, unnecessary, and unhelpful stress. Rather than fall into a rumination trap, hold the situation, mentally speaking, in your mind and try to find other ways to look at it. In other words, reframe. For example:

- If you lost a huge account for your business, rather than focus on all the things that went wrong, choose to think about all that you learned and what you'll do differently as a result of this experience. Yes, there may be consequences. Accept them, know they're temporary. Then, imagine it's two years from now and think about how, in this moment, you'd like to view and characterize this experience looking back on it. The long view has a great way of putting things in perspective.
- If you didn't get selected for a promotion, but your good friend did, it's okay to feel disappointed. Don't, though, let your frustration impact your relationship; work to be

your friend's greatest supporter as he or she transitions. Think about what you would've liked your friend to have done had you earned the promotion. Then, work to be that person for your friend.

- If the fundraising event you created was a total flop—down to the bad food, poor attendance, and missed development goal—remind yourself that in two weeks, this won't be as big a deal as it is today. Be accountable to your planning process and the outcome, while being compassionate with yourself. You might be embarrassed; let that emotion be temporary. With the right spirit, there'll be a chance to look back on this experience and laugh at all the wrong decisions you made, so you can share them for the benefit of the next person's learning.

That last note is key. Our fails present amazing secondhand experiences for someone else. You don't have to hide them; finding the courage to talk about your mistakes can be quite liberating. You'll learn over time, too, that the more you share, the more others share, and the more everyone appreciates the one thing that connects us all on this earth—the reality that no one is perfect, and we all make mistakes.

DISCOVER THE REWARD

Fear and failure are gifts. Like any gift, you've got a choice—you can stuff it away in the closet, unopened; regift it, passing your nerves, insecurities, and blame onto others; or you can open it and discover that what looks frightening and devastating could be exactly what unlocks your potential, just like with a woman we're inspired by.

RISKING IN CAREER AND LIFE: MAYA GABEIRA

Breaking Ground and Reaching New Heights

If you've ever attempted surfing, you know the challenges associated with paddling onto a wave, and then attempting to balance on a board. It's a humbling experience. In fact, it can take hours of practice to do just the simple stuff, like surfing a three-foot wave. Can you imagine, then, the hours and practice and preparation it must take to surf on the big waves? Or, for that matter, the biggest surfing waves known to humankind?

Maya Gabeira knows because she's done it. In 2018, she set the first women's big-wave world record[6] when she rode a sixty-eight-foot wave. And, in 2020, she set the record for surfing the biggest wave again, at seventy three and a half feet—the biggest wave, in fact, any man or woman would surf during the 2020 season.

None of this would've been possible had she allowed her fears and her failures to stop her in her tracks.

In 2013, her first year chasing the biggest waves in the world in Nazaré, Portugal, Maya suffered a major wipeout[7] that not only almost ended her career, it nearly ended her life. The force of the waves broke her right fibula in half, while holding her underwater repeatedly for extended periods of time. At one point, she was floating facedown in the water for more than a minute. Her surf partner pulled her onto the beach and revived her via CPR.

Her recovery took four years and three back surgeries. Pause there for a second. *Four years.* For an athlete, that amount of time away from your sport is soul crushing. It likely made her wonder, too, if surfing competitively was even going to be a possibility for her.

During this period, more devastation followed. She lost all of her sponsors, leaving her with no income to support her future. She dealt with an anxiety disorder and frequent panic attacks, which can feel just as crippling as any physical disorder. She also was publicly scolded and warned by legends of her sport, including Laird Hamilton, who criticized her after her 2013 disaster[8] for not having the skills to attempt big waves.

Yet, during this time, Maya did the work. A different kind of work because of the benefit of her experience.

The obvious ways for Maya to improve after suffering such a massive crash would've included improving her swimming, her strength, her balance, and technique. And, while she spent time on those surfing fundamentals, her ability to make meaning of her crisis and push her thinking beyond the obvious components of her performance are what allowed her to go from the worst experience to best in the world in just seven years.

She knew she needed to grow in creative ways and for that she realized that she also needed to become better not just as an individual, but as a teammate. She transformed by becoming a stronger partner with the hopes of inspiring the best big-wave surfers to want to pair up with her.

So, her recovery wasn't just focused on healing, but on supporting others. With tow-in surfing, athletes go out in teams of two or three, one driving the tow Jet Ski, and one watching to perform rescue if a surfer crashes out, pounded by the incredible force of those monstrous waves. She learned to drive the Jet Ski and perform rescue with excellence, so that when she was healthy enough to surf again, she was seen as a viable surf partner for Sebastian Steudtner, an award-winning big-wave surfer from Germany. Being a better partner allowed her to be better overall.

After Maya's final surgery, she came back, bettering her best in ways the surfing community could never imagine.

We hope you're as inspired by Maya's story as we are; it's a true testament that fear and failure don't have to stop you in your tracks. If you're open to the lessons you can learn, you're able to use them to benefit your life in ways unimaginable. For Maya, that meant surfing. For you? That's the exciting thing—you have the power to define the success that matters to you. The hopes, goals, and dreams you imagine for yourself begin to be available to you when you take a risk, followed by another, in your *Bet on You* journey.

Every leader experiences fear and failure. The best leaders move through the valleys as curious students. Owning their losses, examining them for lessons learned, and working to adapt and apply the takeaways. Embracing risk means preparing for missteps and setbacks, knowing that they allow for the valuable experiences that make the path to greater success more meaningful, joyful, and probable.

PUTTING IT INTO PRACTICE

- Finish the final part of your personal Risk Manifesto at www.leadstar.us/bet-on-you by noting your fears and planning your response to them.

- Become familiar with your fears and war-game them; that way, when you meet, you'll be ready to move beyond them.
- Accept fails as part of your *Bet on You* journey. They're inevitable and need to be appreciated for the great life teachers they are.
- Rare, catastrophic failure is often preceded by warning signs. Look for them. They prevent you from failing too far.
- Know what your go-no-go criteria are; use these criteria to inform your decision to persist or to relent.
- Don't quit when things get difficult—quit when they suck.
- Grief can't be calendared or multitasked; it must be processed in order to grow from your fails.
- When you learn, adapt, and apply the lessons from your failures, you have the opportunity to come back stronger and better.

YOU'VE GOT THIS: ONE SMALL STEP FOLLOWED BY ANOTHER

You've learned throughout your *Bet on You* journey that risk-taking isn't just one big, giant decision that immediately alters your life's direction.

Risk-taking really is about facing uncertainty bravely and making small choices, each day, that move you toward the better dreams and goals you have for yourself that allow you to stretch toward your potential.

You've got so much left to discover about what makes you happy, creates fulfillment, and brings greater meaning to your life. Just think—by taking small risks, you can make something happen every single day for yourself that surprises you and encourages you to take even bigger risks. Small risks like:

- Scheduling time with your supervisor to discuss new ways you'd like to contribute to the team, and how a flexible schedule would support your efforts.
- Finding margin in your life to try new ideas and risk-taking experiments.
- Putting together a draft business plan and meeting with

a commercial loan officer about how much you're quali-
fied to borrow for that business you want to start.

• Making the inquiry at a university to explore what it'll
take to head back to school.

Any of these choices represent an opportunity to further a
dream that's been on your mind. Besides, what's worse than not
taking these types of risks? Looking back on this moment and
wishing you'd had the courage to do one small thing after another.

Risk-taking is a muscle, built through time and with your
confidence and ability to be more self-reliant. As you discover
the small wins your risk-taking can bring, you'll push yourself
toward new areas of exploration that allow you to deepen the
feelings of a winning life that are more enduring and sustainable.

We can't wait for you to discover the rewards your bets on you
bring. People who take risks are, ultimately, more satisfied and
content with their lives than people who play it safe.[1] Besides,
the well-worn path you've been following has reached its limits.
It's time to go off track and embrace a new skill set that will
allow you to be the *more* you want in this life—the more capable,
confident, and better self that meets the high expectations you
have for you.

Only you know where you're holding back and what's holding
you back. These invisible, and often self-made, barriers aren't
serving you. If anything, they're denying you your Ithaka—an
idea we should all be striving for in our life's journey.

WHAT'S YOUR *ITHAKA*?

The poet Constantine Cavafy penned the classic work "Ithaka"
in 1911, a piece that illuminates all that's available to you when
you're intentional about inviting risk-taking into your life each
day.

The poem is inspired by Homer's works, the *Iliad* and *Odyssey,* and centers on the Greek king, Ulysses, a hero of the Trojan War, who's leaving Troy and heading back to his home, Ithaka, an island in Greece. Ulysses's voyage takes ten years.

In that decade, Cavafy reminds Ulysses of the dangers he'll encounter on his journey—*Laistrygonians, Cyclops, angry Poseidon*—only if he gives them attention and carries them in his soul. He encourages Ulysses to detour along the way into ports he's never seen, and to shop and explore—*may you stop at Phoenician trading stations to buy fine things.* Cavafy reminds him, too, that he should take the time on his journey to grow—*visit many Egyptian cities to learn and go on learning from their scholars.*

While Ulysses should never forget that he's heading home, Cavafy reminds him not to rush his return to Ithaka or he'll miss out on the riches the journey avails. *Better if it lasts for years, so you're old by the time you reach the island, wealthy with all you've gained along the way.*

The journey isn't about the destination; the destination was a direction that inspired the learning, growth, discovery, and opportunity. *Wise as you will have become, so full of experience, you'll have understood by then what these Ithakas mean.*

We all have an Ithaka that stirs our senses, entertains our imagination, and creates wonder. It's less of a destination and more of a direction that we walk toward to discover what we were put on this earth to experience and to do.

No two Ithaka journeys are ever alike, but know that you don't have to walk yours alone.

You've developed your Risk Manifesto on your *Bet on You* journey, which can serve as a consistent reminder of the steps you can begin to take to achieve what's most meaningful for you. Keep this by your side so you can understand how to direct your efforts and discover the opportunities that await on your risk-taking journey.

Through your process of rethinking the impact risk-taking

can have on your life, you've done the work of defining what success and significance looks like for you. You've realized a kaleidoscope approach to risking is inspiring because of its whole-life balance. You've taken the time to identify guides—Big Stagers, Champions, and No-Choosers—who are ready to be rallied and claim their spot in your cheering section, so they're there for you when you need them.

You're also invited to be a part of our leadership community that we've been building for decades. Visit www.leadstar.us and learn how to engage with us, as well as with the community of risk-takers who want you to succeed. We're here to support you, and we want you to be assured you've got some great leaders in your corner, too.

You're now risk ready. These next steps are on you. The good news is that you've got this. You're ready to place your most important bets—your bets on you.

Notes

Chapter One

1. Nicola Yoon, *Everything, Everything* (New York: Delacort Press, 2015), p. 68.
2. Q Score: A Q Score or "quotient" (also known as Q-rating) ranks the favorability or appeal of a famous person or item. The higher the Q Score, the more highly regarded the item or person is.
3. Ann Patchett, "The Book of Reese," *Vanity Fair,* March 17, 2020, https://www.vanityfair.com/hollywood/2020/03/the-book-of-reese.
4. In 2021, Reese sold her business to Blackstone Group, a move she made to help her business "tell even more entertaining, impactful and illuminating stories about women's lives globally," https://variety.com/2021/film/news/reese-witherspoon-hello-sunshine-sold-1235032618/.

Chapter Two

1. Janet Champ, Charlotte Moore, Nike advertisement, *Cosmopolitan*, December 1991, https://quoteinvestigator.com/2020/12/08/destined/.

2. Jonathan Coulton, "The Princess Who Saved Herself," Joco website, https://www.jonathancoulton.com/2010/08/16/the-princess-who-saved-herself/.

3. Josh Eells, "Dwayne Johnson: The Pain and the Passion That Fuel the Rock," *Rolling Stone*, April 4, 2018, https://www.rollingstone.com/movies/movie-features/dwayne-johnson-the-pain-and-the-passion-that-fuel-the-rock-630076/.

4. Andrew Nagy, "The Esquire Interview: Dwayne 'the Rock' Johnson," *Esquire Middle East*, July 4, 2018, https://www.esquireme.com/content/28591-the-esquire-interview-dwayne-the-rock-johnson.

5. Luke Norris, "Dwayne Johnson Reveals the Moment He Hit Rock Bottom in His WWE Career," Sportscasting, June 9, 2020, https://www.sportscasting.com/dwayne-johnson-reveals-the-moment-he-hit-rock-bottom-in-his-wwe-career/.

6. The Rock on Instagram: "My career in pro-wrestling was filled with epic highs and epic lows, but all the more important were the lessons it taught me . . . . Always honor (and protect) my relationship with the people. And don't be afraid to step away even when it's counterintuitive. Because there's no harder rock bottom lesson than thousands of fans chanting 'Rocky sucks' in every arena across the country. That was my low. Until I became me. And that became my high," https://www.instagram.com/tv/CAKy_mXF-mv/?utm_source=ig_embed.

7. Josh Eels, "Dwayne Johnson: The Pain and Passion That Fuel the Rock."

8. Friederike C. Gerull and Ronald M. Rapee, "Mother Knows Best: Effects of Maternal Modelling on the Acquisition of Fear and Avoidance Behaviour in Toddlers," *National Library of Medicine* 40(3), March 2002, pp. 279–87, doi: 10.1016/s0005-7967(01)00013-4.

Chapter Three

1. Bob Samples, *The Metaphoric Mind: A Celebration of Creative Consciousness* (Reading, MA: Addison-Wesley Publishing Company, 1976), p. 62.

2. From the Center for Creative Leadership—a nonprofit that has researched heat experiences and their value for development.

Chapter Five

1. "Dolly Parton Explains Why She Didn't Let Elvis Record 'I Will Always Love You,'" Wide Open Country, February 12, 2016 (Updated October 6, 2020), https://www.wideopencountry.com /the-greatest-country-love-song-of-all-time.
2. Marianne Stenger, "How Reverse Planning Can Help You Reach Your Goals," informED, July 13, 2018 (a blog hosted by Open Colleges), https://www.opencolleges.edu.au/informed/features/reverse -planning-can-help-students-reach-goals.

Chapter Six

1. Daniel Kahneman and Angus Deaton, "High Income Improves Evaluation of Life but Not Emotional Well-being," *Proceedings of the National Academy of Sciences* 107(38), September 2010, 16489 –16493, https://www.pnas.org/content/107/38/16489.

Chapter Seven

1. Bill Watterson, *The Calvin and Hobbes Lazy Sunday Book* (Kansas City, MO: Andrews McMeel Publishing, 1989), p. 60.
2. Alan Paul, "John Oates Stands Alone," *Wall Street Journal*, October 9, 2020, Weekend Confidential, https://www.wsj .com/articles/john-oates-stands-alone-11602258995.
3. Helen Brown, "Daryl Hall & John Oates: 'Michael Jackson told me at Live Aid that "I Can't Go For That" had inspired "Billie Jean,"'" *The Independent*, October 2, 2020, https://www.independent.co.uk /arts-entertainment/music/features/hall-oates-interview-michael- jackson-hunter-s-thompson-maneater-lyrics-tour-b694510.html.
4. Craig Rosen, "John Oates Discusses His Famous Mustache and Favor- ite Musical Memories," Yahoo! News, July 8, 2016, https://www .yahoo.com/news/john-oates-discusses-his-famous-mustache -and-171741210.html.

Chapter Eight

1. Jessica Rovello, "5 Ways Katie Lydecky, Michael Phelps, and Other Olympians Visualize Success," *Inc.*, https://www.inc.com/jessica-rovello/five-steps-to-visualize-success-like-an-olympian.html.
2. Oprah Winfrey, "What Oprah Learned from Jim Carrey," Oprah.com, October 12, 2011, https://www.oprah.com/oprahs-lifeclass/what-oprah-learned-from-jim-carrey-video.
3. Hope Perlman, "5 Secrets of Sustainable Success by Billy Jean King," *Psychology Today*, October 7, 2013, https://www.psychologytoday.com/us/blog/unmapped-country/201310/5-secrets-sustainable-success-billy-jean-king.
4. Kelly McLaughlin, "Here Are the Chances of Getting Bitten by a Shark While You're Swimming at the Beach," Insider.com, July 21, 2018, https://www.insider.com/shark-attacks-what-are-odds-of-getting-bitten-2018-7.
5. Patricia Mazzei, "Opioids, Car Crashes and Falling: The Odds of Dying in the U.S.," *New York Times*, January 14, 2019, https://www.nytimes.com/2019/01/14/us/opioids-car-crash-guns.html.
6. David Stubbings, "68-ft Wave Surfed by Maya Gabeira Confirmed as Largest Ridden by a Woman as She Receives Two Awards," October 1, 2018, Guinness World Records, https://www.guinnessworldrecords.com/news/2018/10/68-ft-wave-surfed-by-maya-gabeira-confirmed-as-largest-ridden-by-a-woman-as-she-r-542488.
7. Lou Boyd, "Maya Gabeira: I Just Thought, 'This Is It, I'm Going to Die,'" *The Red Bulletin*, January 31, 2019, https://www.redbull.com/gb-en/theredbulletin/Maya-Gabeira-interview-surfing.
8. Lou Boyd, "Maya Gabeira: I Just Thought, 'This Is It, I'm Going to Die.'"

Conclusion

1. Jennifer Warner, "Are Risk Takers Happier?" WebMD, September 19, 2005, https://www.webmd.com/balance/news/20050919/are-risk-takers-happier.

Index

Angie Morgan and Courtney Lynch met in the Marine Corps and have since applied their leadership lessons learned through their work at their consultancy, Lead Star, and their books, the *New York Times* bestseller *SPARK* and *Leading from the Front*.

Angie Morgan

Angie is a dynamic, creative thought leader who knows how to unlock the capability and talent of leaders at all levels. Angie's competitive nature and motivation to win shows up in every client engagement as she inspires others to be their best. She holds a BA and an MBA from the University of Michigan. Angie's an avid athlete and mother of two boys, and she loves nothing more than riding her road bike throughout her hometown—Traverse City, Michigan.

Courtney Lynch

Courtney is a big-picture thinker whose life's mission is to support individuals as they become the best leaders they know.

Clients turn to Courtney for her in-the-moment advice and breadth of real-world experiences. She holds a BA from North Carolina State University and a JD from the College of William & Mary. Courtney's passions are skiing, reading, and spending time with her three kids and husband, Patrick.